Editor
Eric Migliaccio

Illustrator
Mark Mason

Cover Artist
Brenda DiAntonis

Editor in Chief
Ina Massler Levin, M.A.

Creative Director
Karen J. Goldfluss, M.S. Ed.

Art Production Manager
Kevin Barnes

Art Coordinator
Renée Christine Yates

Imaging
Rosa C. See

Publisher

Mary D. Smith, M.S. Ed.

Social Studies Lessons Using **Graphic Organizers**

Grades 7–8

Teach content and thought process simultaneously

Promote inferential and evaluative thinking

Improve critical and analytical thinking skills

Enhance knowledge of early civilizations, world history, and American history

CD-ROM

Author

Debra J. Housel, M.S. Ed.

Teacher Created Resources, Inc.
6421 Industry Way
Westminster, CA 92683
www.teachercreated.com
ISBN: 978-1-4206-8187-1
© 2008 Teacher Created Resources, Inc.
Made in U.S.A.

Teacher Created Resources

Table of Contents

Introduction

Social Studies Lessons Using Graphic Organizers will save you time and effort. It contains complete lessons that meet the standards for your grade level in history and geography. There are five lessons about early civilizations, nine lessons about world history, and eight lessons about American history.

Each lesson uses a different graphic organizer. Thus, if you do all the lessons in this book and never use another graphic organizer, your students will have worked with 22 different graphic organizers. This provides significant exposure to these important educational tools.

Graphic organizers show the organization of concepts and the relationships among them. They offer a clear depiction of data that research has proven is more memorable than pages of notes. They show students "how it all fits together," which is much more effective than having them try to memorize bits of data without thoroughly understanding the context. Showing how information is organized helps students—especially English-language learners and those with reading disabilities—focus on content instead of semantics and grammar.

Compelling Reasons to Use Graphic Organizers

Research shows that graphic organizers actually improve students' creative, analytical, and critical-thinking skills. Why? Graphic organizers help students of all ages to process information. Processing information is a complex skill requiring the ability to identify essential ideas, to decide which details are relevant and which are irrelevant, to understand how information is structured, and to figure out how data relates to other information or situations. This demands the use of such higher-level thinking skills as making decisions, drawing conclusions, and forming inferences.

Substantial amounts of research support the fact that graphic organizers increase the understanding and retention of critical information for all students. This means that using graphic organizers may meet the needs of the many different learners in your classroom without the time-consuming task of individualization.

The visual element inherent in graphic organizers supports three cognitive-learning theories: dual-coding theory, schema theory, and cognitive-load theory.

- **Dual-coding theory** acknowledges that presenting information in both visual and verbal form improves recall and recognition. Graphic organizers do both effectively.

- **Schema theory** states that a learner's prediction based on his or her background knowledge (schema) is crucial for acquiring new information. This is why readers have a hard time comprehending material in an unfamiliar subject even when they know the meaning of the separate words in the text. Graphic organizers' ability to show relationships clearly builds upon and increases students' schema.

- **Cognitive-load theory** stresses that a student's short-term memory has limitations in the amount of data it can simultaneously hold. Since any instructional information must first be processed by short-term memory, for long-term memory (schema acquisition) to occur, instruction must reduce the short-term memory load. Thus, teaching methods that cut down on the demands of short-term memory give the brain a better opportunity to facilitate activation of long-term memory. Graphic organizers fit the bill perfectly.

Graphic organizers are appearing more often in standardized tests and state assessments. Giving your students practice with the variety of graphic organizers offered in this book can help them to achieve better scores on these assessments.

Introduction *(cont.)*

How to Use This Book

The lessons in *Social Studies Lessons Using Graphic Organizers* are designed to be used where they fit in your curriculum. Whenever you start a new unit, check to see if one of these lessons will work with your topic. The reading level for each was determined using the Flesch-Kincaid formula and may be indicated in the lesson. The lessons within each section are presented in chronological order, and it would be logical to do them sequentially.

The lessons often require that you make a transparency and student copies of the graphic organizers located on the CD. Any other necessary materials will be stated in the lesson. They will be things such as highlighters, poster board, scissors, and glue. When writing on the transparency, you may want to use different colors to differentiate between specific sections. This is another way to help your students visualize data.

The graphic organizers give as much space as possible for the students to write. However, if some of your students have large handwriting, make a transparency of the blank graphic organizer and display it on the overhead. Then have a school aide or the students tape a sheet of construction paper where the overhead projects and copy the format onto the paper. This will give them more room to write.

If you are just starting to use graphic organizers, you may worry that they are time-consuming. Keep in mind that it is time well-spent. Graphic organizers provide meaningful instruction that gives your students an advantage in comprehending and remembering data. By using graphic organizers you are teaching not just content but thought processes. Your students are learning how to learn—an invaluable skill that will serve them well for the rest of their lives.

Be Flexible and Creative

The graphic organizers included in this book have many uses; they are not limited to these lessons or content areas. Most of these graphic organizers can be used or modified to fit the needs of other lessons or subjects. Sometimes a student will self-advocate by asking you to make copies of a certain kind for use in other areas. You may find that a challenged student enjoys and learns best using one particular type. Be flexible and creative in your use of graphic organizers.

If you have a class that really enjoys graphic organizers and you feel confident in their use, you can evaluate student learning by letting the students create their own graphic organizers. You may be pleasantly surprised at your students' ability to make meaningful graphics that show interrelationships in a more effective way than they could explain in writing.

Note: In the passages in this book, all dates are written as "BCE" ("Before the Common Era"; formerly "BC") and "CE" ("in the Common Era"; formerly "AD").

 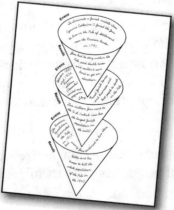 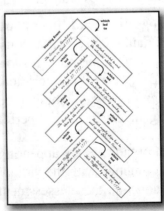

Standards Correlation Chart

Each lesson in this book meets at least one of the following standards and benchmarks, which are used with permission from McREL. Copyright 2006 McREL. Mid-continent Research for Education and Learning. Address: 2250 S. Parker Road, Suite 500, Aurora, CO 80014. Telephone: 303-337-0990. Website: *www.mcrel.org/standards-benchmarks*

World History Standards and Benchmarks	Pages
Standard 3. Understands the major characteristics of civilization and the development of civilizations in Mesopotamia, Egypt, and the Indus Valley	
• **Benchmark 1.** Understands environmental and cultural factors that shaped the development of Mesopotamia, Egypt, and the Indus Valley	8–15
• **Benchmark 2.** Understands the role of economics in shaping the development of Mesopotamia, Egypt, and the Indus Valley	8–15
Standard 4. Understands how agrarian societies spread and new states emerged in the third and second millennia BCE	
• **Benchmark 3.** Understands what archaeological evidence (e.g., bronze vessels) reveals about Chinese history during the Shang Dynasty	21–24
• **Benchmark 4.** Understands the significance of advancement in tools & weapon technology	8–28
Standard 5. Understands the political, social, and cultural consequences of population movements and militarization in Eurasia in the second millennium BCE	
• **Benchmark 3.** Understands significant individuals and events in Egyptian civilization	12–15
Standard 6. Understands major trends in Eurasia and Africa from 4000 to 1000 BCE	
• **Benchmark 1.** Understands the emergence of civilizations in Southwest Asia, the Nile Valley, India, China, and the Eastern Mediterranean and how they represented a decisive transformation in human history	8–15, 21–24
• **Benchmark 2.** Understands why geographic, environmental, and economic conditions favored hunter-gatherer, pastoral, and small-scale agricultural ways of life rather than urban civilizations in many parts of the world	8–11, 21–24
• **Benchmark 3.** Knows the fundamental inventions, discoveries, techniques, and institutions that appeared from 4000 to 1000 BCE; and understands the significance of bronze technology	8–15, 21–24
Standard 8. Understands how Aegean civilization emerged and how interrelations developed among peoples of the Eastern Mediterranean and Southwest Asia from 600 to 200 BCE	
• **Benchmark 1.** Understands the political framework of Athenian society	16–20
• **Benchmark 4.** Understands elements of Alexander of Macedon's legacy	16–20
Standard 9. Understands how major religious and large-scale empires arose in the Mediterranean Basin, China, and India from 500 BCE to 300 CE	
• **Benchmark 2.** Understands influences on the economic and political framework of Roman society	16–20
• **Benchmark 3.** Understands fundamental social, political, and cultural characteristics of Chinese society under early imperial dynasties	21–24
Standard 11. Understands major global trends from 1000 BCE to 300 CE	
• **Benchmark 1.** Understands the importance of "classical civilizations"	16–20
• **Benchmark 2.** Understands the development of large regional empires	16–20

Standards Correlation Chart *(cont.)*

World History Standards and Benchmarks	Pages
Standard 15. Understands the political, social, and cultural redefinitions in Europe from 500 to 1000 CE • **Benchmark 5.** Understands the role of Norse peoples in the development of Europe	33–36
Standard 22. Understands the growth of states, towns, and trade in sub-Saharan Africa between the 11th and 15th centuries • **Benchmark 1.** Understands the development of the empires of Mali and Songhay	29–32
Standard 24. Understands the expansion of states and civilizations in the Americas between 1000 and 1500 • **Benchmark 2.** Understands cultural and economic elements of North American and Mesoamerican civilizations	25–28
Standard 26. Understands how the transoceanic interlinking of all major regions of the world between 1450 and 1600 led to global transformations • **Benchmark 1.** Understands the impact of the exploratory and commercial expeditions in the 15th and 16th centuries	37–40
Standard 27. Understands how European society experienced political, economic, and cultural transformations in an age of global intercommunication between 1450 and 1750 • **Benchmark 1.** Understands early influences on the Scientific Revolution & the Enlightenment • **Benchmark 3.** Understands significant social and cultural changes that took place during the Renaissance	41–44 41–44
Standard 32. Understands the causes and consequences of political revolutions in the late 18th and early 19th centuries • **Benchmark 2.** Understands events and ideas that influenced the course of the French Revolution • **Benchmark 5.** Understands the political and ideological objectives of Latin American independence movements	45–48 45–48
Standard 34. Understands how Eurasian societies were transformed in an era of global trade and the emergence of European power from 1750 to 1870 • **Benchmark 2.** Understands political conditions in Russia during the reign of Catherine the Great	49–52
Standard 36. Understands patterns of global change in the era of Western military and economic dominance from 1800 to 1914 • **Benchmark 1.** Understands major developments in science and the industrial economy	57–60
Standard 37. Understand major global trends from 1750 to 1914 • **Benchmark 2.** Understands major patterns of long-distance migration of Europeans, Africans, and Asians, as well as causes and consequences of these movements	53–56, 81–84
Standard 41. Understands the causes and global consequences of World War II • **Benchmark 3.** Understands the influence of Nazism on European society and Jewish culture	49–52
Standard 43. Understands how post-World War II reconstruction occurred, new international power relations took shape, and colonial empires broke up • **Benchmark 1.** Understands factors that brought about the political and economic transformation of Western and Eastern Europe after World War II • **Benchmark 2.** Understands post-war relations between the Soviet Union, Europe, and the United States	61–64 61–64

Standards Correlation Chart (cont.)

American History Standards and Benchmarks	Pages
Standard 1. Understands the characteristics of societies in the Americas, Western Europe, and Western Africa that increasingly interacted after 1450	
• **Benchmark 1.** Understands the rise and decline of the Mississippian mound-building society	25–28
• **Benchmark 3.** Understands the influence of Islam in Western Africa in the 15th and 16th centuries	29–32
Standard 3. Understands why the Americas attracted Europeans, why they brought enslaved Africans to their colonies, and how Europeans struggled for control of North America and the Caribbean	
• **Benchmark 1.** Understands the cultural and environmental impacts of European settlement in North America	65–68
Standard 6. Understands the causes of the American Revolution, the ideas and interests involved in shaping the revolutionary movement, and reasons for the American victory	
• **Benchmark 3.** Understands the strategic elements of the Revolutionary War	69–72
• **Benchmark 4.** Understands the impact of European countries and individual Europeans on the American victory	45–48
Standard 9. Understands the United States territorial expansion between 1801 and 1861 and how it affected relations with external powers and Native Americans	
• **Benchmark 3.** Understands the social and political impact of the idea of Manifest Destiny	73–76
Standard 16. Understands how the rise of corporations, heavy industry, and mechanized farming transformed American society	
• **Benchmark 1.** Understands influences on business and industry in the 19th century	81–84
• **Benchmark 3.** Understands influences on the development of the American West	73–76
Standard 17. Understands massive immigration after 1870 and how new social patterns, conflicts, and ideas of national unity developed amid growing cultural diversity	
• **Benchmark 1.** Understands the background and experiences of immigrants of the late 19th century	49–56, 81–84
Standard 18. Understands the rise of the American labor movement and how political issues reflected social and economic changes	
• **Benchmark 1.** Understands the conditions affecting employment and labor in the late 19th century	81–84
• **Benchmark 2.** Understands reactions to developments in labor in late 19th century America	81–84
Standard 19. Understands federal Indian policy and United States foreign policy after the Civil War	
• **Benchmark 2.** Understands the causes and consequences of the Spanish-American War	77–80
Standard 21. Understands the changing role of the United States in world affairs through World War I	
• **Benchmark 3.** Understands the United States' intervention in World War I	85–88
• **Benchmark 4.** Understands the impact of the United States' involvement in World War I	85–88
Standard 25. Understands the causes and course of World War II, the character of the war at home and abroad, and its reshaping of the U.S. role in world affairs	
• **Benchmark 8.** Understands how minority groups were affected by World War II	89–92
Standard 30. Understands developments in foreign policy and domestic politics between the Nixon and Clinton presidencies	
• **Benchmark 2.** Understands major foreign policy events and how they influenced public opinion of the administrations from Nixon to Clinton	61–64, 93–96

Early Civilization

Day 1

1. Obtain maps showing ancient Mesopotamia (including Phoenicia and Sumer).

2. Introduce unfamiliar vocabulary by writing the words on the board or overhead and giving students an opportunity to provide definitions for the ones they know:

   ✧ **arable**—suitable for growing crops

   ✧ **irrigation**—manmade system to supply water to fields

   ✧ **cuneiform**—a type of writing that involves triangular marks made on damp clay tablets

   ✧ **scribes**—people (usually men) whose job it was to read and write

   ✧ **innovation**—new idea or invention

   ✧ **ziggurat** (ZIG-oo-rat)—a temple with a number of stories and having a broad ascent winding around the structure, giving the appearance of a series of terraces

3. Make a transparency and student copies of "Mesopotamia: Civilization Begins" on page 9.

4. Display the transparency, covering all but the title. Ask your students to tell you what they already know about Mesopotamia. What can they tell from the title?

5. Distribute the student copies of the passage. Uncover and read aloud the first paragraph. Stop to have your students identify and use highlighters to mark the important vocabulary. Underscore the words on your transparency. Discuss the paragraph with the class.

6. Uncover and read aloud the second paragraph and then stop to identify and highlight the vocabulary. Discuss the paragraph. Continue in this way until you have read the whole passage.

7. Show your students a map of ancient Mesopotamia and where Sumer, Phoenicia, and Carthage were located.

8. Then show your students on a map where the places mentioned in the passage are located in the modern world: the Tigris River, the Euphrates River, Iraq, the Mediterranean Sea, Carthage, and the Lebanon Mountains. This is an important step in helping your students to understand why ancient history is relevant to today's world.

Day 2

1. First, make a copy of the "Write All About It" graphic organizer on page 11. Next, write the words at the top and the three column headings shown on the completed graphic organizer on page 10. Then, make student copies of the organizer on which you've written.

2. Distribute the student copies of the graphic organizer. Read the directions to the class.

3. Have your students get out the passage from yesterday. They can use the passage to help them sort the words in the box into the three topics (column headings).

4. Circulate to be sure that the students sort the words correctly. Use questioning to guide them to move words they've placed incorrectly.

5. Your students may use the passage to help them compose their three paragraphs. For those students who feel crowded by the space left for the paragraphs on the graphic organizer, suggest that they use a separate sheet of paper or the back of the graphic organizer.

6. Remind your students that since they have the passage to which to refer, you will expect correct spelling and capitalization.

7. Collect the paragraphs and check for understanding.

Mesopotamia: Civilization Begins

The world's first known civilization began in a place we call the Fertile Crescent. Ancient Mesopotamia was the area surrounding the Tigris and Euphrates Rivers in the Middle East. In a region where most of the land is desert-like, this area had arable land and water. Within Mesopotamia there were different territories with unique cultures, including Sumer and Phoenicia.

Sumer, also known as the Cradle of Civilization, developed in what is now Iraq. The Sumerians lived there between 4500 and 3000 BCE. They made the first plow and the first wheel. They created irrigation systems to water their crops. They had a mathematical system based on the number 60. In fact, they created the 60-minute hour we still use.

Sumerians may have had the world's first system of writing, too. Scribes carved cuneiform into wet clay tablets. It took a young man 12 years to learn how to read and write these marks. This system spread all over southwestern Asia. Many of these tablets still exist, and people have learned much about ancient societies from them.

The Sumerians lived in buildings made from bricks of sun-dried mud. Since such bricks do not last forever, no complete example of their architecture remains. But some ruins do, and from them people have figured out what the original buildings looked like. The most important building in any city was the ziggurat. Located in the center of a city, some of these step-type pyramids towered seven stories high. Each level was smaller than the one below it, so the top of the ziggurat was the smallest level. It had a shrine to the god who watched over that city.

At that time people bartered, or traded, in order to get the goods they wanted. This was both time-consuming and difficult. First, people had to find what they wanted. Then they had to hope that the owner would want to trade for what they had to offer. About 4000 BCE the Sumerians invented cone-shaped tokens. They put them into clay envelopes and sealed them. Then they made marks indicating how many were inside. Traders used these in the marketplace. This was a first step toward what would later become money.

The Phoenicians lived in the northern part of Mesopotamia. They did not have good farmland, but they did have an abundant supply of cedar trees in the Lebanon Mountains. They used these trees to build magnificent ships that sailed throughout the Mediterranean Sea. They became great sea traders. Between 1000 and 700 BCE the Phoenicians built colonies all over the Mediterranean, including Carthage in North Africa in 814 BCE. (Carthage would later be a serious threat to Rome.)

These ancient people were the first to outfit the rich and famous. They discovered how to make purple die from shellfish and created beautiful fabric. This purple cloth was so rare and expensive that only royalty wore it. The Phoenicians are best remembered for their 22-letter alphabet. Since they had colonies in so many places, this alphabet spread throughout the ancient world. It was later adopted by the Romans and is similar to our 26-letter alphabet.

Early Civilization

Cradle of Civilization	Iraq	Euphrates	alphabet
Tigris	60	royalty	mud bricks
Mediterranean	wheel	cuneiform	ships
shrines	purple	Fertile Crescent	colonies
clay tokens	plow	ziggurats	Lebanon Mountains

- Put each word in the box into *one* of the three groups below.
- Each group may have a different number of terms.
- Write a paragraph using all the words in the first group.
- Then write a second paragraph using all the words in the second group.
- Do the same for a third paragraph.

Mesopotamia	Sumer	Phoenicia
Tigris	Iraq	Lebanon Mountains
Euphrates	shrines	alphabet
Fertile Crescent	clay tokens	Mediterranean
	60	purple
	wheel	ships
	plow	colonies
	mud bricks	royalty
	cuneiform	
	ziggurats	
	Cradle of Civilization	

Paragraphs:

Mesopotamia, or the Fertile Crescent, was where the first societies began because this land could be farmed. It was located around the Tigris and Euphrates Rivers.

Called the Cradle of Civilization, Sumer was located in what is now Iraq. The people there made the wheel and the plow. Their buildings were made of mud bricks. They made ziggurats for shrines to their gods. They also created cuneiform writing and a numerical system based on the number 60. Their clay tokens made trade easier.

Phoenicia was another civilization in the area. They didn't have much farmland, but they had lots of cedar trees in the Lebanon Mountains. So they built ships and sailed around the Mediterranean, forming new colonies. Their alphabet was similar to ours, and they made purple dye. Only royalty could afford their purple cloth.

- Put each word in the box into *one* of the three groups below.
- Each group may have a different number of terms.
- Write a paragraph using all the words in the first group.
- Then write a second paragraph using all the words in the second group.
- Do the same for a third paragraph.

Paragraphs:

_____

_____

_____

_____

_____

Day 1

1. This lesson offers a very condensed version of Egyptian history, so you can use it to introduce the topic of Ancient Egypt or as a wrap-up leading to the unit test.

2. Prior to doing this lesson, gather books, encyclopedias, and other reference materials about ancient Egypt. If possible, get Internet access. On a map, show your students Lower and Upper Egypt, the Nile River, Nubia, the Red Sea, Assyria, Persia, and Rome.

3. Introduce unfamiliar vocabulary:
   - **domesticated**—made tame
   - **papyrus**—a material on which to write made from the pith (stems) of the water plant of the same name
   - **famine**—time of starvation
   - **diagnostic medicine**—the science of figuring out what's physically wrong with a person and then making a treatment plan

4. Make and distribute student copies of "Ancient Egypt: Land of Pharaohs and Pyramids" on page 13. The passage is written at an 8.6 reading level.

5. Discuss the passage with the class. Encourage them to identify ideas about ancient Egypt about which they would like to know more.

6. Make and distribute student copies of the "Key Ideas" graphic organizer on page 15.

7. Assign students to teams of three. Have the students skim the passage to come up with a relevant phrase or sentence that starts with the different letters, or computer keys, of the alphabet. Allow students to use words beginning with the letters *Ex* for the *X* key. The students should select a scribe who will fill in the "Key Ideas" graphic organizer, which will be submitted for a group grade. Each team fills in as many boxes as possible within a time limit you set.

Day 2

1. Show your students how to use the reference materials you have gathered.

2. The teams must complete the "Key Ideas" graphic organizer using these resources within a time limit you set. They must have facts for at least 23 of the 26 keys.

3. Have each team identify one fact that they want to share with the class. It should be something they consider unique, surprising, or particularly interesting.

4. One member of each team stands and states the fact to the class. This team member cannot be the team scribe.

5. Discuss the facts the students found interesting.

Day 3

1. Make sure that each student has a copy of his or her team's graphic organizer.

2. Have the students independently write at least four paragraphs about ancient Egypt using the facts contained on the graphic organizer. When they have finished, have the students staple the graphic organizer to their composition.

3. Collect the graphic organizers and essays to check for understanding.

Ancient Egypt: Land of Pharaohs and Pyramids

The first people settled in the Nile Valley sometime around 5500 BCE. Each year, the Nile River flooded. This left rich silt for several miles inland along its banks. The people grew crops and domesticated cattle, sheep, goats, and donkeys.

About 3100 BCE Upper Egypt (south) and Lower Egypt (north) merged to form one nation, and the capital city of Memphis was built. The king, or pharaoh, had supreme power. He was seen as a god because the people thought that he was a descendant of the sun god, Re. People began using hieroglyphs, or picture writing, to make records.

Around 2686 BCE Egypt entered a 500-year period of peace. During this time, the first step pyramid was built at Saqqara. Later Khufu's Great Pyramid at Giza and many of the other pyramids were constructed. The pyramids were the pharaohs' burial sites. Each ruler was mummified before being placed in his tomb. Ancient papyrus scrolls from this time prove that the people knew how to make a kind of paper and ink.

About 2181 BCE a climate change resulted in years of insufficient Nile River floods. This caused a major famine. Civil war erupted, dividing Egypt into two kingdoms. After 60 years, Mentuhotep II reunited the nation and built a new capital at Thebes. Then his army took over the Sinai Peninsula and parts of Nubia (Africa). Archaeologists have uncovered evidence that the Egyptians practiced diagnostic medicine during this time.

In 1674 BCE Hyksos kings took control of Lower Egypt. The pharaoh kept some power at Thebes, but it took nearly a century for the Egyptians to regain control. Then they seized more land. Shortly after this, Egypt reached the height of its power and wealth as tributes from conquered nations flowed into its treasury. One of the few female pharaohs, Hatshepsut, ruled for 22 years. To command respect, she always appeared dressed as a male pharaoh. Later, Akhenaten tried to force his people to worship one god. They had to go along with him. But as soon as he died, Tutankhamun (Tut) reinstated the old gods.   Although he ruled for less than 10 years, you probably know Tut's name. Discovery of his gold-filled tomb has made him famous.

About 1085 BCE the Nubians conquered the nation, and Egypt lost its status as a world power. Next, Assyrians conquered the area in 715 BCE, and then the Persians took over in 525 BCE. The Persian King Darius built a canal from the Nile River to the Red Sea.

Egyptians took back power in 404 BCE, but by 332 BCE the Greek warrior Alexander the Great made Egypt a part of his empire. The pharaoh stayed on the throne only by completely accepting Alexander's leadership. During this time, the Rosetta Stone was carved. This stone, which had the same message written in three languages, helped archaeologists to decode hieroglyphs.

In 30 BCE the Roman Empire annexed Egypt. For the first time in their 3,000-year history, Egyptians abandoned their culture. They adopted Rome's. Ancient Egypt was no more.

Write phrases or sentences about the topic. Start each one with a different letter. You can use words that start with the letters *Ex* for the *X* key. You might not find a sentence for every letter.

Early Civilization

A	Akhenaten tried to force Egyptians to worship one god
B	burial site of Tutankhamun has made him famous
C	civil war split the nation into two kingdoms in 2181 BCE
D	Darius, the Persian king, built a canal joining the Red Sea and Nile River
E	every pharaoh was made into a mummy after his or her death
F	floods from the Nile River made the land good for growing crops
G	gold (as tribute) from nations it conquered made Egypt grow rich
H	Hyksos kings took over part of Egypt in 1674 BCE and held control for 100 years
I	
J	
K	Khufu's mummy was laid inside the Great Pyramid at Giza
L	Lower Egypt was in the north
M	Memphis was the capital city
N	Nile Valley is where people first settled in Egypt around 5500 BCE
O	
P	Persians took control in 525 BCE
Q	Queen Hatshepsut was a female pharaoh who dressed like a male
R	Romans annexed Egypt in 30 BCE
S	Saqqara is the site of the first step-pyramid
T	Thebes was a secondary capital
U	Upper Egypt was in the south
V	
W	warrior king Alexander the Great made Egypt part of his empire in 332 BCE
EX	examples of three languages carved on the Rosetta Stone let people finally decode Egyptian hieroglyphics
Y	
Z	

Write phrases or sentences about the topic. Start each one with a different letter. You can use words that start with the letters *Ex* for the *X* key. You might not find a sentence for every letter.

Early Civilization

A	
B	
C	
D	
E	
F	
G	
H	
I	
J	
K	
L	
M	
N	
O	
P	
Q	
R	
S	
T	
U	
V	
W	
EX	
Y	
Z	

Early Civilization

1. Introduce unfamiliar vocabulary:
   - **philosopher**—a person who offers theories on questions in ethics, science, and logic
   - **republic**—a political system in which power rests with the citizens entitled to vote and is exercised by representatives chosen by them
   - **plebeians**—commoners
   - **ruthless**—showing no mercy
   - **undisputed**—generally agreed upon; without question
   - **martyred**—killed (usually in a brutal way) because of being part of a group or cause
   - **annihilate**—destroy completely
   - **formidable**—having awesome size, strength, or influence

2. Make and distribute student copies of "Ancient Greece and Rome: More Alike than Different" on pages 17–18. The piece is written at a 7.8 reading level, so pair the students accordingly and have them read the first four paragraphs together.

3. Reconvene as a whole class and discuss Ancient Greece.

4. Have the students return to their partners and read the rest of the passage.

5. Reconvene as a whole class to discuss Ancient Rome.

Day 2

1. Have available books on Ancient Greece and Rome. Decide in advance if you want your students to select Greece or Rome or if you want to assign one of those societies for the poster project. More information is given in the passage about Rome than Greece, so you may want to assign Rome to ELL students or those for whom research might be challenging.

2. Make and distribute student copies of the "Poster Planner" graphic organizer on page 20. Explain that the students will take information from both the passage and the books to create a unique poster about Ancient Greece or Ancient Rome.

3. Have each student use a highlighter on the passage to identify the facts that they want to include on the poster. At least two facts on the poster must from come from another source.

4. Post this list of steps where your students can refer to it:
   - Decide what facts to include.
   - Work in pencil on the organizer. Make a note of pictures you plan to find or draw.
   - Do all drawings in pencil. Later make the poster colorful with markers or colored pencils.
   - Make light pencil lines with a ruler so that you will have straight lines on which to write.
   - Write all information in pencil. Go over it with a black felt-tip marker.
   - Erase all stray marks and the lines on which you wrote.

Days 3–5

1. Students prepare their posters. Circulate to help them.

2. Record the grade for each poster on the back, and then display it in the hall.

Note: After the first time you do this lesson, ask two of your students if you may keep their completed posters to show as examples for the next time you teach it.

Ancient Greece and Rome:
More Alike than Different

From 800 BCE to 145 BCE Greece was an advanced civilization in the Mediterranean. The nation had many city-states, the most important of which were Sparta and Athens. Sparta had an amazing army. All boys belonged to the city-state at birth. At the age of 7, they left home to begin their military training. All Spartan men had to serve in the army until the age of 60. It was the highest honor to die in battle for Sparta, and Spartan soldiers would fight to the death rather than be taken as prisoners. All men and women, regardless of age, had to work hard, be physically fit, and never give up. Today if we say that someone lives a "Spartan lifestyle," we mean that he or she has self-discipline.

Athens was a center for art, architecture, and education. Located right on the sea, it had ships used for trade or war. The famous philosopher Aristotle lived in Athens from 384–233 BCE. He wrote about logic and experimentation. His ideas formed the foundation of scientific methods.

At first all city-states were *oligarchies*, which means that a few rich families ruled. Then Athens formed the first democratic government in 508 BCE. This government made choices based on the majority vote of its male citizens. (Women and slaves did not vote and had few rights.) This political development would affect the world for centuries to come.

The Greek general Alexander the Great had a strong army in 334 BCE. He never lost a major battle as he built a gigantic empire. He took over Persia, Egypt, and India, spreading Greek knowledge to these areas. He named multiple cities "Alexandria" throughout this territory.

Meanwhile Rome, another great culture, was growing in strength. When the Romans conquered Greece in 146 BCE, they absorbed Greek knowledge. They borrowed their beliefs and architecture, too. This explains the many similarities between the two ancient cultures.

Around 753 BCE a man named Romulus had built the city of Rome. He was the first of many kings. In 509 BCE Rome became a republic, which meant that senators made the laws and decisions. Roman males elected these senators. Rome maintained this kind of government for nearly 500 years.

The Romans had four social classes: citizens, plebeians, slaves, and noncitizens. Only the men who owned land were citizens. Plebeians were men without land. They could vote but not speak before the Senate. Noncitizens were women and foreigners. They had few rights. Slaves, often captives won in war, had no rights.

A strong military made the Roman Empire powerful. The soldiers were ruthless and determined to hold and expand the Empire's territory. People were terrified of the Roman army. They often threw down their weapons rather than fight against them. The Roman Empire spread throughout the Mediterranean region, North Africa, and the Middle East, bringing its ideas, way of life, and the Latin language to millions.

Ancient Greece and Rome:
More Alike than Different *(cont.)*

Beginning in 264 BCE, Rome fought the Punic Wars against Carthage, Africa. In 146 BCE the Romans defeated Hannibal of Carthage, and Rome became the undisputed world power.

In 59 BCE Julius Caesar, a Roman general, took over Gaul (now France). Caesar then triumphed in a Roman civil war and became Rome's undisputed leader. But the senators, who thought that Caesar was acting like a king, killed him in 44 BCE. This led to another civil war. Then, Octavian, Caesar's son, defeated the armies of Antony (of Rome) and Cleopatra (of Egypt) in 31 BCE. He reunited Rome and took over Egypt. Four years later, he was renamed Augustus and made the first Roman emperor. This ended the Roman Republic and began a 200-year period of peace for Rome. During this time, emperors created the world's first census (for tax purposes), an extensive system of stone roads and aqueducts (for moving water), and laws that form the basis of Western legal systems, including the rule that you are innocent until proven guilty.

The Romans worshipped many gods. They tolerated other religions and usually let conquered peoples keep their faith. However, they hated Christians. Christians would not make animal sacrifices to the Roman gods. The Romans were afraid that this would offend the gods, who would then cease to protect their Empire. Christians who would not give up their faith were martyred. They were stoned, beheaded, or thrown to hungry lions. Thousands crowded into the arena and cheered as the lions tore them apart. When Christians were blamed for the fire that destroyed most of the city of Rome in 64 CE, efforts to annihilate them intensified.

Then, in 312 CE, Roman Emperor Constantine saw a sign in the sky and became a Christian. In 313 the Edict of Milan made Christianity acceptable. And since it was the emperor's religion, it became preferred to other faiths. After 200 years of persecution, being a Christian was now advantageous.

In 330 Constantine moved Rome's capital to the city of Byzantine and renamed it Constantinople (now the city of Istanbul in Turkey). In 1054 the Christian church split into the Roman Catholic Church (in Rome) and the Eastern Orthodox Church. The Roman Catholic Church grew into a formidable religious and military power in Europe.

The Roman Empire was huge. The Persians in Asia, the Berbers in North Africa, and Germanic invaders from Europe tried to seize Roman territories. It was impossible to effectively fight enemies in different areas at the same time. In 476 CE the Empire split in two. The Western Empire quickly fell apart. The Eastern, or Byzantine, Empire lasted another 1,000 years.

The Roman Empire ended long ago, yet it still affects our lives. Although Latin is no longer spoken, it is the basis for the Italian, French, Spanish, and Portuguese languages. Many English words have Latin roots. We read Roman myths and use Roman numerals. Most of the planets in our solar system are named after Roman gods or goddesses.

Title and Your Name

Ancient Greece
by Jamie Rodriguez

Picture and Fact

Aristotle lived in Athens
from 384–233 BCE.
His ideas formed the
foundation of
scientific methods.

**Central Image/Fact of
Greatest Importance**

the birthplace of
Western civilization

Picture and Fact

Greek general Alexander
the Great conquered Persia,
Egypt, and India and
spread Greek knowledge.

**Startling or
Interesting Fact**

Athens,
a Greek
city-state,
had the world's
first democracy
in 508 BCE.

**Startling or
Interesting Fact**

Sparta,
a Greek
city-state,
claimed
ownership of
all newborn males.

Optional Fact or Picture

The
Olympic
games first began in
Greece in 776 BCE.
Only men could
compete—and they
were nude!

Picture and Fact

Greeks worshipped gods
and goddesses. Zeus was the
chief god of the Greeks.

Picture and Fact

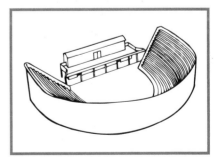

Greeks wrote plays and
performed them in
outdoor amphitheaters.

Early Civilization

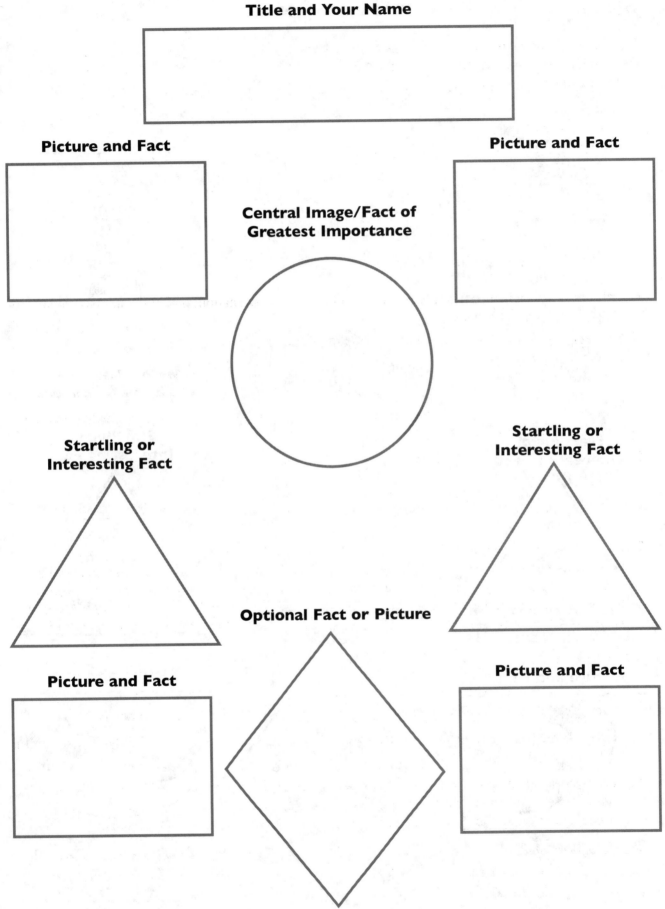

Title and Your Name

Picture and Fact

Picture and Fact

Central Image/Fact of Greatest Importance

Startling or Interesting Fact

Startling or Interesting Fact

Optional Fact or Picture

Picture and Fact

Picture and Fact

Day 1

1. This would be a good introduction to a unit about ancient China. Before doing this lesson, have available books, encyclopedias, access to the Internet, and other reference materials for students to investigate this topic.

2. Make student copies of "Ancient China: Birthplace of New Ideas" on page 22. Introduce unfamiliar vocabulary:

   ❖ **Paleolithic**—the Stone Age, which appeared first in Africa and was marked by the steady development of stone tools (and later antler and bone artifacts), engravings on bone and stone, sculpted figures, and paintings and engravings on cave walls

   ❖ **Neolithic**—the New Stone Age (also called the Stone Age's last phase), marked by animal domestication, agriculture, and the making of pottery and fabric

   ❖ **millet**—a grass with small seeds cultivated in the Far East and in southern Europe; people make cereal from it

   ❖ **dynasty**—when one family line holds all the power in a nation; in China, the family claimed the "Mandate of Heaven"

   ❖ **reign**—the period during which a specific person or family rules

3. This article is written at a 7.6 reading level. Take this into account when you have the class read it.

4. Discuss the article. Also, be sure to point out to your students on a map the two major landmarks mentioned in the article: the Himalayan Mountains and the Great Silk Road.

5. Make a transparency and student copies of the "K-W-L Chart" graphic organizer on page 24. Display the transparency and distribute the copies.

6. Ask your students for three important facts about ancient China from the passage. Use the information to fill in the "I Know" column.

7. Ask students what they wonder about ancient China. Write three of their questions on the transparency in the "I Wonder" column. These questions must have substance; they cannot be ones answered by a "yes" or "no" or a name, date, or number. Each class member can choose to research these questions or questions of his or her choice (as long as three are researched). Explain that they are to write the answers in the "I Learned" column of the organizer.

Days 2–3

1. Give your students time to investigate the books and other materials you've gathered. Depending on the complexity of the questions, you may need to give them time over several days.

2. Create a large K-W-L chart on a piece of poster board. List the questions posed by the class from the transparency.

3. Reconvene as a whole group. Ask volunteers to provide the answers and write them across from the questions on the chart. Have students who pursued their own questions offer what they learned and add it to the class chart. Keep the class K-W-L chart on display throughout the unit.

Early Civilization

Ancient China: Birthplace of New Ideas

China has the oldest continuous recorded history on Earth. About 1.6 million years ago there were hunting-and-gathering societies in China. Paleolithic hunters and gatherers made tools by chipping stones. They created tiny blades with very sharp points and tied them to sticks to create spears. This practice continued through the early Neolithic Age. This marked the time when people first settled down in villages, domesticated animals, and planted crops.

The earliest known village in China had about 100 houses, several workshops, and many animal pens clustered around a big central plaza.   It dates back to 6500 BCE, making it about 8,500 years old. Yet pieces of 10,000-year-old pottery prove that there were human societies even before that. And we know that at least 10,000 years ago the Chinese grew rice and millet. The people of this time made items of jade, ceramic, stone, and bone.

Ancient China was an advanced civilization. Its people created many things hundreds of years before the people in Europe did. Over time, Europeans have received the credit for many of these things. For example, the Chinese actually made the first magnetic compass, and they made a fishing reel 1,400 years before anyone else. Due to the Himalayan mountain chain that separated them from much of the rest of the continent, the Chinese had little to do with the rest of the world. This means that they were mostly developing new things without building upon the ideas of others.

About 2000 BCE the Chinese began to make bronze. At that time it was a rare and costly metal. The items made were just used in rituals and religious ceremonies. Sometime during the Han Dynasty (206 BCE and 220 CE), the people began using bronze to make household items and tools.

The first dynasty in China was the Shang. They ruled from 1600 BCE until 1100 BCE. During their reign, the Chinese created many things, including silk cloth, horse-drawn chariots, and a calendar. Then the Zhou took over and ruled for nearly 900 years. Of all the dynasties, it lasted the longest. During this time both paper and paper money were invented. Both the Shang and the Zhou Dynasties made bronze tools and beautiful works of art.

Over time, the dynasty system weakened. Small armies began to fight one another. The nation split into many small territories. When the Han Dynasty reunited China into one large empire in 206 BCE, the nation's influence on surrounding nations grew. The Great Silk Road was completed. This was the first time China and the nations of the Middle East, Africa, and Europe were connected. Even so, it would be more than 1,000 years before the Western world knew about many of the Chinese inventions. Why? Few people traveled between Europe and China. It was a long, hard, dangerous trip. In 1274 an Italian named Marco Polo went to China and lived there for 24 years. When he returned home, he wrote a book about the amazing things he saw there. But almost no Europeans believed him.

K-W-L Chart

I Know

- China has the oldest continuously recorded history.

- The Himalayan Mountains separated China from the rest of the world.

- Dynasties ruled China (one family line ruling for centuries).

- The longest-lasting dynasty was the Zhou.

- Marco Polo visited China, but Europeans didn't believe what he told them about the nation.

I Wonder

- What caused the end of the Zhou Dynasty?

- When and why was the Great Wall constructed?

- Why has China developed so few innovations in recent centuries?

I Learned

- Over time, the Zhou's power waned, until they were just figureheads. The nobles rebelled and declared themselves rulers of different sections of China. Then, Zin Shi Huang's army defeated the Zhou and began the Zina Dynasty.

- Most of the Great Wall dates from the Ming Dynasty (1368–1644). The emperor ordered it built in the late 1400s due to Mongol attacks. Older walls were incorporated into the Great Wall, which protected China from minor attacks but did not work against huge invasions, cannon fire, or attacks from the sea.

- About 1433 CE the Ming Dynasty decided China should no longer interact with Europeans. All but one seaport closed to European trade, and things remained that way until 1842, when Great Britain forced the Chinese to trade with them. During the 400 years of Chinese isolation, the rest of world had continued to interact and exchange knowledge. When people share ideas, innovation moves at a rapid pace.

Early Civilization

K-W-L Chart

I Learned

I Wonder

I Know

Mississippian Mound-Builders

Day 1

1. Explain to your students that architecture often reflects the beliefs of its builders. Thus, you can learn things about a culture from its architecture.

2. Introduce unfamiliar vocabulary:

   ✧ **ensure**—to make certain

   ✧ **reign**—the period during which a specific person or family rules

   ✧ **tributaries**—streams and rivers that feed into a larger river

3. Make student copies of "The Mississippians: Landscape Architects" on page 26. It is dense text, so read the article as a class.

4. After reading, you may want to show photos of the Mississippian mounds. Many are available in encyclopedias and on the Internet (do an image search).

5. Show maps of the territory controlled by the Mississippian people. Also point out to your students the modern-day states and places mentioned: Cahokia, Illinois; Spiro, Oklahoma; Moundville, Alabama; and Etowah, Georgia.

6. Make a transparency and student copies of the "Web" graphic organizer on page 28. Distribute the student copies and display the transparency.

7. As a class, identify and transfer the major understandings from the article onto the lines of the web. The completed graphic organizer is shown on page 27.

8. Ask your students what questions they still have about the Mississippians. Make a class list on chart paper.

9. As a class, research the answers to one of the questions. Use this opportunity to show your students how to find answers on the Internet or in an encyclopedia. It's important to discuss the search term (keyword) under which to look for information. If one search term doesn't work, what others can they try? What kinds of websites are reliable sources?

Day 2

1. Group the remaining questions on the chart into pairs. Put the students into small groups and assign each group one pair of questions. Give students time to do research to discover the answers.

2. After the groups compose their answers on the backs of their graphic organizers, have a volunteer from each record the information on a large piece of poster board.

3. Discuss the questions and their answers with the class.

Early Civilization

The Mississippians: Landscape Architects

From 800 CE until 1500 CE, a Native-American culture thrived in what is now the Midwest and Southeast United States. The Mississippian Mound Builders' civilization stretched from present-day Wisconsin to the Gulf of Mexico and to the Atlantic Ocean in what is now Georgia.

The Mississippians built the cities of Spiro in present-day eastern Oklahoma, Moundville in Alabama, and Etowah in northern Georgia. Each city had a central plaza. At different times, this plaza served as a marketplace, a festival site, and a sports arena. The biggest city was Cahokia in what is now Illinois. It had more than 85 mounds; and, at its height, more than 30,000 people lived there.

Huge mounds of varying sizes dotted the land. The mounds had houses built on their flat tops. Tall, steep stairs led to a walled enclosure that surrounded the home. Homes were made of mud bricks and topped with grass-thatched roofs. The tallest mounds belonged to those with the highest social status. Mounds also marked borders and burial plots. How did they make all these mounds? Men carried baskets of dirt by hand. It was a time-consuming process. Often workers spent their lifetimes building a mound that they never saw completed.

Monks Mound, the biggest in Cahokia, still exists. It has two terraces and a massive base that is 25 percent larger than the base of the Great Pyramid of Giza in Egypt. Chief Great Sun lived atop this mound. The people believed that he had the power to control the forces of nature to ensure good weather and plentiful harvests. It took more than two centuries of daily labor to build his mound, which towered 100 feet above the other mounds in the city. During his reign, Cahokia's population was greater than that of any European city. After Cahokia was abandoned in 1250, it wasn't until 1781 that another North American city (Philadelphia) had a larger population.

The Mound Builders are considered a prehistoric people, since they did not develop a system of writing. Nor did they have the wheel. But they were skilled potters and stoneworkers and wore beads, necklaces, and earrings. They perfected the bow and arrow. For nearly 500 years, they cultivated large plots of land, growing enough corn, squash, and beans to feed enormous populations. They also traded among themselves, using the Mississippi River and its tributaries for travel.

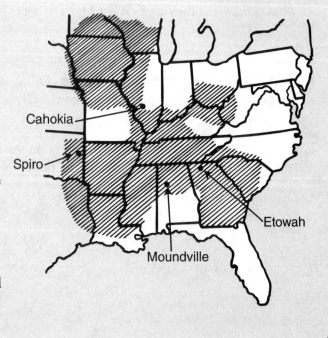

No one knows why the Mississippian Mound Builders' culture declined. Since it covered such a vast area, even a huge flood would not have killed everyone. Most signs of them had vanished by the time the Spanish explorer Hernando DeSoto arrived in the area in 1540.

Web

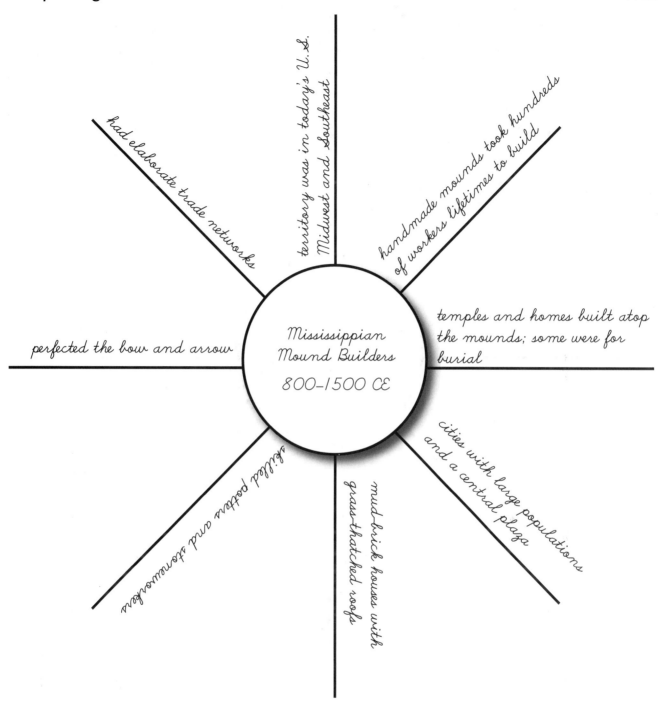

had elaborate trade networks

territory was in today's U.S. Midwest and Southeast

handmade mounds took hundreds of workers lifetimes to build

perfected the bow and arrow

Mississippian Mound Builders 800–1500 CE

temples and homes built atop the mounds; some were for burial

skilled potters and stoneworkers

mud-brick houses with grass-thatched roofs

cities with large populations and a central plaza

(**Note:** These are just example questions; use the ones your students have.)

Did the Mississippians ever fight among themselves? Did they take scalps?

Yes, they did fight among themselves: skeletons found in burial mounds have arrowheads in them. Also, their artwork shows scalping and beheading of enemies.

What are the theories as to the disappearance of the Mississippian culture?

There are two theories: perhaps they fought an internal war over natural resources or died from diseases brought by Old World explorers. Neither theory has strong support.

Early Civilization

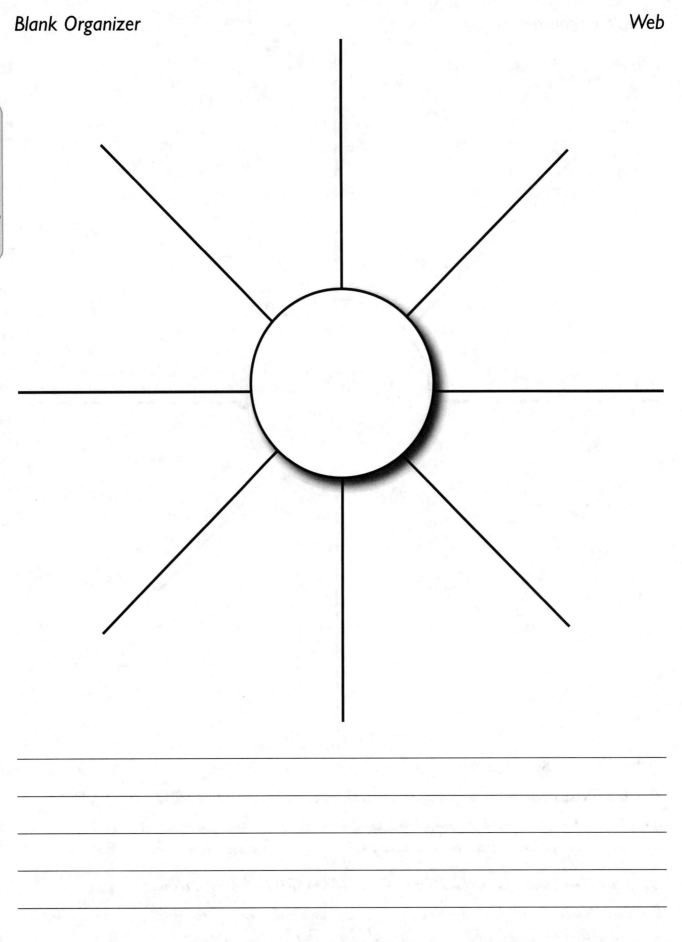

_____

_____

_____

_____

_____

_____

Day 1

1. Introduce unfamiliar vocabulary:

   ✧ **ultimatum**—a warning that action will be taken unless certain demands are met
   ✧ **convert**—to change (religious beliefs, etc.)
   ✧ **retaliated**—took revenge for a perceived wrong
   ✧ **economy**—a nation's production and consumption of goods and services and its supply of money
   ✧ **devout**—deeply religious
   ✧ **mansa**—emperor or sultan
   ✧ **pilgrimage**—journey to a place, usually for religious reasons
   ✧ **inventory**—entire stock held by a merchant
   ✧ **circulation**—movement through (such as money in an economy)
   ✧ **flourished**—thrived
   ✧ **publicized**—made public; made many people aware

2. Make and distribute student copies of "West African Kingdoms: Empires Built of Salt and Gold" on page 30. The passage is written at a 6.5 reading level. Have your students read it.

3. Discuss the article. Also, be sure to point out to your students on a map the places mentioned in the article: the Niger River; the Sahara Desert; Cairo, Egypt; and Mecca, Saudi Arabia.

4. Make a transparency and student copies of the "Square Venn Diagram" graphic organizer on page 32.

5. Display the transparency and distribute the copies.

6. As a class, fill in the graphic organizer together for the kingdoms of Ghana and Mali, writing things that are similar in the intersecting box and the things unique to each kingdom beneath its own heading. (See the completed graphic organizer on page 31.)

Day 2

1. Make and distribute more student copies of the "Square Venn Diagram" graphic organizer.

2. Have available Internet access, books, and other resources about the Songhay Empire (also spelled *Songhai*).

3. Pair the students. Have your students research the Songhay Empire and then use the "Square Venn Diagram" organizer to compare it to the Mali Empire.

3. Have the students compose a summary of the information they wrote on the graphic organizer. They should have at least two paragraphs: one to emphasize how the two empires were alike, and one to tell how they were different.

4. The students should discuss, compose, and revise this summary. Then each pair submits the summary to you for a grade.

Extension: Today the majority of the world's diamonds come from mines in Africa. Have your students research how the diamond trade has affected the people of Africa.

World History

West African Kingdoms: Empires Built of Salt and Gold

Historians believe that the first civilization in the West African area was comprised of farmers living along the Niger River. Around 300 CE these farmers banded together to form the nation of Ghana. Then they presented a united front to the nomads who wanted to let their animals graze on the farmers' crops.

Ghana had a vast supply of gold; and the Sahara Desert, rich in salt, lay to its north. Back then, salt was almost as valuable as gold. Why? People needed it in their diets. They also used it to keep food from spoiling. Today, salt is inexpensive. But back then it was not unusual for people to pay a pound of gold for a pound of salt!

Like many civilizations long ago, Ghana's rulers grew rich through trade. They controlled all the trade routes for both salt and gold. By 800 CE nearly all traders moving between northern and southern Africa went through Ghana. Each trader who entered Ghana paid a tax on the goods he carried in. Then he paid another tax on the goods he carried out. Ghana's soldiers also had iron weapons that were superior to the weapons of others living in the area.

As the kingdom of Ghana grew larger, Arab traders entered its borders. They brought with them their religion, Islam. In 1076 Muslim warriors gave Ghana's leader, Tenkamenin, an ultimatum: accept Islam as the state religion or be ruined. He refused to force his people to convert. The Muslims retaliated by blocking the country's trade routes, which weakened the nation's economy. The nearby kingdom of Mali seized this opportunity to attack and take over Ghana.

The Malians did not resist Islam. At first, they accepted the religion just to keep peace with the Arab traders. Over time, they became devout believers. Mali's most famous leader was Mansa Musa. He made a pilgrimage to the holy city of Mecca. In 1324 he started out, traveling slowly by camel caravan. More than 60,000 people went with him, all wearing or carrying gold. By the time he reached the Middle East, news of his magnificent traveling party had people lining the streets for a glimpse. Musa was so rich that he dropped a gold nugget into every outstretched palm! He bought merchants' whole inventories. He left so much gold in circulation in Mecca that its value fell. In Cairo, Egypt, he also distributed so much gold that its value did not recover for a dozen years.

West Africans had had no form of writing. Musa invited Arab scholars to come and teach his people to read. He wanted them to read the Qu'ran, the holy book of Islam. Art, architecture, and learning flourished under his leadership. However, after his death, Mali weakened and was absorbed by the Songhay Empire.

Musa's visit had publicized the wealth of West Africa. For centuries greedy rulers looked for an opportunity to take these resources for themselves. In 1591 the ruler of Morocco in North Africa overthrew the Songhay with guns—weapons the Songhay had never before seen and for which they had no good defense. Thus ended the Golden Age of West Africa.

Kingdom of Mali

accepted Islam and got along with Muslim traders

Mansa Musa—most famous leader—made pilgrimage to Mecca in 1324

world became aware of his kingdom's wealth from this trip

Musa had Arab scholars teach people to read and write

art and architecture flourished

after he died, Songhay took over kingdom

held vast supplies of salt and gold

leaders very wealthy

controlled the trade routes for both salt and gold

eventually overthrown by other African leaders

Kingdom of Ghana

made iron weapons; had strong military

traders paid taxes on goods carried in and out

Tenkamenin refused to convert to Islam, so Muslims blocked trade routes in 1076

economy ruined, and Mali overthrew the kingdom

World History

1. Write the word "Vikings" on the board. Have your students do a quick write. Give them one minute to write everything they know about the topic. This writing is to stimulate background schema and will not be shared with anyone else. This technique lets students approach the reading with greater confidence by making them realize that they already know something about the topic.

2. Introduce unfamiliar vocabulary:

    ✧ **spindle**—a slender rod with tapered ends used in conjunction with a spinning wheel to spin wool or flax by hand

    ✧ **descendants**—the blood relatives of a specific ancestor

3. Make and distribute student copies of "Master Sailors: The Vikings" on page 34. This passage is written at a 5.3 reading level, so your students should be able to read it independently.

4. After your students have read the article, ask them to compare their quick-write notes with the passage. What did they already know that was correct? Did they have any misconceptions?

5. Make and distribute student copies and display a transparency of the "Balancing Bar" graphic organizer on page 36.

6. Explain to your student that when reading expository text, they need to determine the main idea and supporting details. They can envision the main idea as a bar balanced on a top of a column. Draw the analogy that the column (details) holds up (supports) the main idea. Without the column, the bar would fall—just as without details, the main idea is merely a statement without any proof.

7. Of course there is a main idea and details given in every paragraph of a well-written nonfiction article. You want your students to find the one overall idea that underlies this entire piece. This is a complex process, so guide the students in the steps:

    • First, have them reread the passage looking for the common thread in all the paragraphs. (*ships*)

    • Then, once your students have recognized this fact, ask them, "What was the importance of the Vikings' ships?" (*They invented the keel, which enabled ships to sail further, faster, and safer than ever before and let them set up colonies in far-away places such as Greenland. Ships were so important that they were used as coffins for the rich.*)

    • Ask them to state the main idea, incorporating all these ideas: The Vikings' beliefs and culture were based upon their magnificent ships, which were the finest vessels of their time.

    • Now, have the students find the statements in each paragraph that support that main idea.

8. Complete the graphic organizer as a class.

9. For homework, have the students use their graphic organizers to write a short summary (approximately three paragraphs) of the information they outlined.

Master Sailors: The Vikings

The Vikings were a group of people whose sailors explored the North Atlantic Ocean from 700 to 1100 CE. They lived in the countries now called Denmark, Norway, and Sweden.

Since they lived so close to the sea, they used water as their main way to get around. Over the years they became expert shipbuilders. They designed a way to build ships that let them go farther and faster than any ships had gone before. How? They invented the keel. This long, narrow piece of wood was attached beneath the ship and helped to steer the boat. Even better, it kept the ship from rolling when it was struck by a wave. This let the boat move faster. Because it could get places more rapidly, the ship could go much farther without stopping for new supplies of food and water. At that time, Viking ships were the finest in the world.

Each ship had striped square sails and a front that curved up into a wooden carving of a dragon's head, which allowed people to identify a Viking ship while it was still miles away. Out in the ocean, the ships used the wind to fill their huge wool sails. However, on a river, people rowed the boat. Each ship had 15 or 30 pairs of oars. In a narrow boat, one man would work a pair of oars. In wider ships, one man worked each oar.

The ships let the Vikings use sea routes to trade throughout Europe and explore the Arctic and Atlantic Oceans. They sailed so far across the Atlantic that they actually landed in North America nearly 500 years before Columbus did. Leif Ericsson set sail from his home in Norway around 1000 CE. He discovered Canada and named it Vinland. Then he went home and told others about the place. The next year, men and women set out to build homes in the new land. However, the Native Americans did not want the people there and repeatedly destroyed the newcomers' villages. Around 1005 the discouraged colonists gave up. They left and never returned.

A spindle dug up in Newfoundland, Canada, proves that this happened. A woman used it to spin wool into yarn 1,000 years ago. Only people in Norway used this kind of spindle. This simple tool proves that the Vikings reached the New World long before Columbus ever set sail.

Viking ships also carried settlers to Greenland, which is icy. They just called it Greenland to get people to go there. They brought people to Iceland, as well. The Vikings' descendants still live in both of these countries.

All Vikings were proud of their ships. When they died, rich Viking men and women had a ship for a coffin. Besides the corpse, the ship held the dead person's belongings, such as jewelry and weapons. The Vikings buried these ships with the belief that they would give the people a safe passage to the land of the dead.

Main Idea

The Vikings' culture and beliefs were based upon their magnificent ships, which were the finest vessels at that time.

Support

Vikings lived in Denmark, Norway, and Sweden and explored the North Atlantic Ocean from 700 to 1100 CE.

They invented the keel, which helped them to steer, kept the ship from rolling at sea, and helped their vessels go faster and farther.

Their ships had dragon heads and square sails. The sails were used at sea, but on rivers, people rowed with oars.

Vikings used sea routes to trade throughout Europe.

Leif Ericsson discovered America about 1000 CE, but Viking colonists were driven away by the Native Americans.

Vikings colonized Greenland and Iceland.

Rich Vikings and their belongings were buried in ships in order to journey to the land of the dead.

World History

World History

Main Idea

[ ]

Support

1. Explain that you are going to read about the first trip around the world. Point out to your students on a globe or a world map the places that will be mentioned in the passage: Spain, the coast of Africa, Brazil, the coast of South America, the Strait of Magellan, and the Philippines.

2. Introduce unfamiliar vocabulary:

   ✧ **unwittingly**—unaware of the facts; unintentionally

   ✧ **mutiny**—an open rebellion by sailors against their captain

   ✧ **scout ahead**—to make a detailed search in order to report back to a larger group

   ✧ **inlet**—a place where a river enters the sea

3. Make and distribute student copies of "Magellan's Journey Around the World" on page 38. It is written at a 4.9 reading level, so your students can read it independently.

4. Discuss the article by asking such questions as the following:

   • "How do we know so many details about Magellan's trip around the world?"
   (*One of the surviving sailors kept a journal.*)

   • "Look at a map. Which two cold oceans did Magellan's fleet not sail through? Why didn't they go through these oceans?" (*They did not go through the Arctic Ocean—this body of water is at the top of Earth and completely out of the way of the path the fleet took. They also did not go through the Southern Ocean (which surrounds Antarctica) because it was too far to the south. The fleet sailed across the Atlantic to reach the Strait of Magellan, then across the Pacific, skirted along the Indian Ocean and up the coast of Africa (Atlantic Ocean) to return to Spain.*)

   • "Would you have like to have been a sailor on one of Magellan's ships that went around the world? Explain why or why not."

   • "How did Magellan's voyage change the world?" (*He proved the world was round; his men made maps that other captains used; Europeans sent out explorers to learn more about the lands visited during his trip, more Europeans came to the New World, causing the death and displacement of native peoples; etc.*)

5. Discuss the reason why the fleet was stalled near the equator for three weeks. This region is called "the doldrums" because there is almost no wind. Explain that centuries ago sailors couldn't do anything about being stuck in the doldrums because their ships moved only via sails (*wind power*). The trade winds are located about 700 miles away on both sides of the equator. Their ship had to drift far enough north or south to pick up the trade winds in order to start moving again.

6. Make a transparency and student copies of the "Follow in the Footsteps" graphic organizer on page 40. Display the transparency and distribute the student copies.

7. Have the students refer to the passage to determine eight major events on Magellan's historic voyage. (Refer to the completed graphic organizer on page 39.)

8. As a class, fill in the graphic organizer.

World History

Magellan's Journey Around the World

Five hundred years ago, sailing—even in familiar waters—was an adventure. There were no radios, weather reports, or good maps. Sailors were on their own, and many died in shipwrecks. So little was known about Earth and its seas that no one was certain that the world was round. At that time it was just a theory. Then Ferdinand Magellan led more than 235 men on a voyage. They were the first crew to sail around the world and the first Europeans to cross the Pacific Ocean.

Magellan had sailed to the Spice Islands for King Manuel of Portugal. When the king turned against Magellan, Magellan went to King Charles of Spain. Magellan wanted to try to reach the islands from the other direction. King Charles agreed to pay for his voyage. That made King Manuel so angry that he sent three men to interfere. Unwittingly, Magellan hired them as three of his four captains. They set sail in September 1519. Magellan commanded the *Trinidad*. The other ships in his fleet were the *San Antonio, Concepción, Victoria,* and *Santiago*.

Along Africa's coast strong thunderstorms battered the fleet. Next, they drifted for three weeks. They had to wait for the weather to change and wind to blow. In the meantime, the ships started to leak, and the heat made water and wine barrels burst. Some of their food rotted. At last, they headed southwest. One captain planned a rebellion, or mutiny. He wanted to seize command. Instead, Magellan put him in chains.

In November they reached Brazil's shore and rested there. On Christmas Day they started going down the South American coast. On the way they explored each river and bay. They moved slowly and ended up in a cold, barren place on April 1. (In the Southern Hemisphere, it is autumn in April.) The three captains rose up against Magellan. He killed two and left the third on the shore in chains.

The crew built huts and set up camp. For food, they caught black-and-white "geese" that couldn't fly (penguins) and "legless sea wolves" (sea lions). They sent the *Santiago* south to scout ahead. When it was wrecked, only two of its crew made it back to camp. The fleet set out again in August 1520. In October they found a bay. Magellan sent two ships to explore it. A violent storm began that lasted for two days. The ships took shelter in a small inlet. They found that it was a long waterway. Although it had land on both sides, the water was salty. They had discovered the Strait of Magellan at the tip of South America. They came back and got the rest of the fleet. For the first time in history, people sailed from the Atlantic to the Pacific Ocean. It took one month.

The weather was awful, and the new captain of the *San Antonio* turned his ship around and fled. It took the remaining ships from November 1520 until March 1521 to cross the Pacific and reach the Philippines. There, Magellan was killed when he tried to force the natives to become Christians. But those in his crew who survived sailed one ship back to Spain. When they arrived in September of 1522, just 18 men had survived the three-year trip. One sailor had kept a log about this adventure that proved that the world is round.

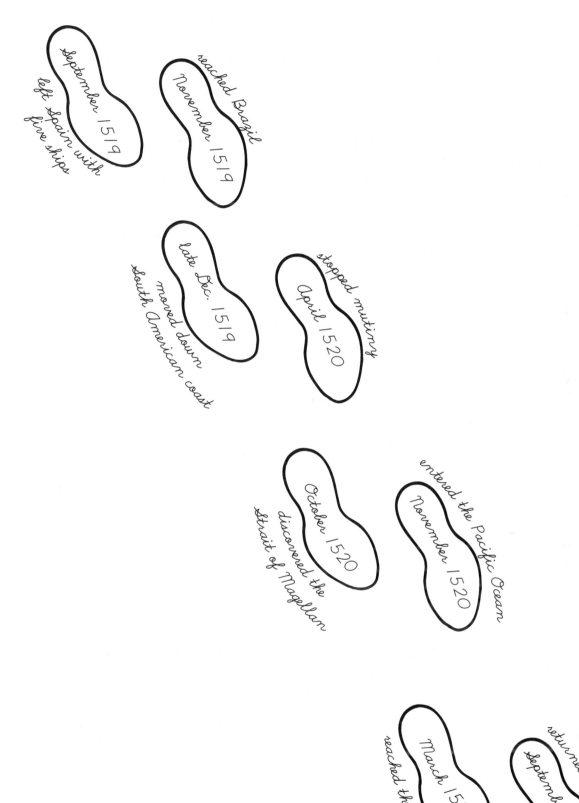

World History

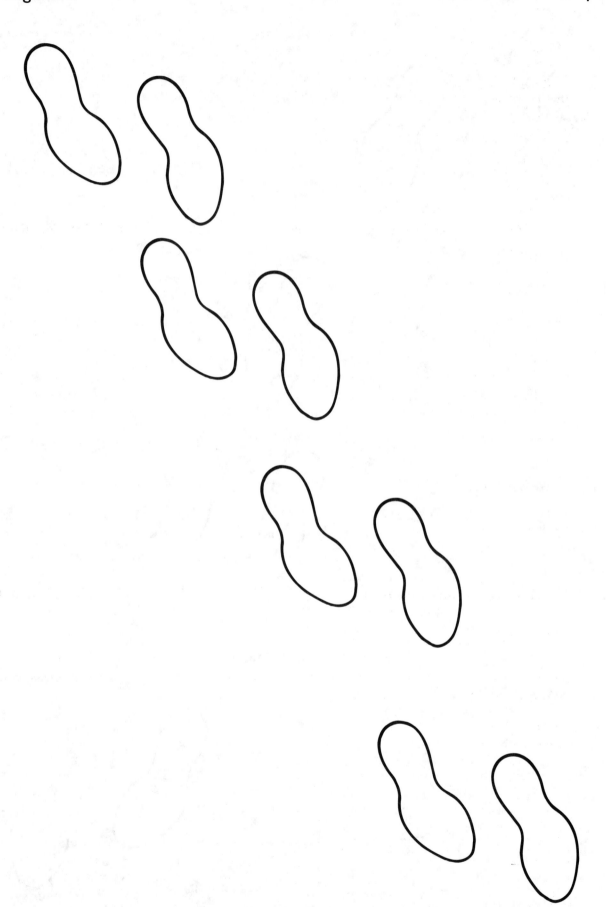

1. Tell your class that a hot topic is a topic about which many people are interested or are discussing. It may be a subject of some controversy. Ask your students to name some current hot topics.

2. Explain that 550 years ago, a new way to make books was a hot topic. Four hundred years ago, a discovery about how our solar system works was a hot topic, as well.

3. Introduce unfamiliar vocabulary:

   ✧ **medieval**—of the Middle Ages, the time period in Europe between the fall of the Roman Empire and the Renaissance, spanning from about 500 CE to about 1350; considered a time when little progress was made in art, literature, and knowledge

   ✧ **Renaissance**—a time period in Europe starting in the 14th century and lasting into the 17th century in which there was a renewal in art, literature, and knowledge. The Renaissance period was the transition from the medieval to the modern world.

   ✧ **institution**—major organization

   ✧ **heretic**—a person whose beliefs go against traditional religious teachings

4. Before reading the passage, be sure that your students understand that the progression of knowledge was brought to a virtual standstill when barbarians overthrew Rome in 476 CE. After that, even fewer people knew how to read or write. The Roman Catholic Church was the richest and most powerful institution in the world and had its own standing army. Anyone who knew how to read or write did so because they were taught in one of its monasteries (for men) or convents (for women). Thus, the Church controlled almost all learning in Europe.

5. Make and distribute student copies of "Invention and Discovery During the Renaissance" on page 42. It is written at a 4.8 reading level. Have your students read it.

6. Discuss the passage. Ask the students to discuss anything they find surprising.

7. Make a transparency and student copies of the "Hot Topics" graphic organizer on page 44. Display the transparency and distribute the copies. Explain that the shape of a chili pepper shows that the subject is "hot."

8. Write the words *printing press* inside the top of the upper chili pepper. That's the topic. Have students identify three important understandings about the printing press and its effect on the world. Write this information on the body of the chili pepper.

9. Write *solar system* inside the top of the lower chili pepper. Have students identify three important understandings about the solar system and its discovery's effect on the world. Write this information on the body of the chili pepper. (Depending upon the needs of your class, you can have them do this as a class or have them do it independently.)

Extension: Make a copy of the blank "Hot Topics" graphic organizer. Write a key topic from the Renaissance in the top of each chili pepper and then make copies. Have the students do research to fill in three important points about these topics.

Invention and Discovery During the Renaissance

Before 1450 every book was copied by hand using a quill pen, which was a bird feather dipped in ink. Monks spent years making one copy of a book. Once they finished, they started to make another copy. This made books cost so much that only the rich could own them. With so few books, ideas and knowledge spread slowly.

Johannes Gutenberg worked in Germany's mint making coins. He heated gold or silver and poured the liquid metal into molds. When the metal cooled, it formed a coin. This gave Gutenberg the idea to make separate letters out of metal. In 1428 he started working in secret on his project. It took him years to make hundreds of pieces of type. He made each letter of the alphabet and punctuation marks. He used these letters to form words. He set the words in rows in a tray. Then he rolled ink onto the "type." Next he pressed paper against it. (This is how it got the name "printing press.") The ink on the type pieces came off on the paper. He hung the page up to dry. Later, a person sewed the pages in order and put a fabric cover on the book. In 1450 he printed his first book, a 641-page Bible. He made about 300 copies.

Gutenberg's printing press was one of the most important inventions in history. Ideas could be shared faster and easier than ever before. Not long after he did this, scientists began to question how the world worked. When they published their findings, they ran into conflict with the Roman Catholic Church, the institution that controlled almost all learning in Europe.

The Church taught that the universe was a hollow ball—like the inside of a soccer ball. Earth was in the center. The sun, the moon, and the planets went around it. About 1520, Nicolaus Copernicus figured out that this was wrong. He watched the way that the moon and planets move in the night sky. Although he could not prove it, he could tell that Earth and all the planets went around the sun. The Church did not like Copernicus's ideas. It restated that Earth was the center of the universe—and anyone who said otherwise was a heretic and would be executed.

Galileo Galilei knew about Copernicus's ideas and agreed with him. But he had no way to prove it until he met a man in 1609 who showed him a new Dutch invention: a crude telescope. Galileo improved it with curved glass lenses that made things appear 32 times bigger. He used his telescope to watch the night sky and kept records of the motion of the moon and planets. By 1613, he knew that all the planets revolved around the sun.

When Galileo wrote about his findings, the Church attacked him. He waited for things to settle down and repeated his findings in another book 20 years later. This time the Church sentenced him to burn at the stake. It also ordered the burning of all of his books. Galileo did not want to die, so he said that he had written lies. The Church put him under house arrest for the rest of his life to prevent him from sharing his ideas with others. But Galileo had changed the world. He had made a useful telescope and showed other scientists the importance of making careful observations and keeping records. And he caused people to question the Church's teachings.

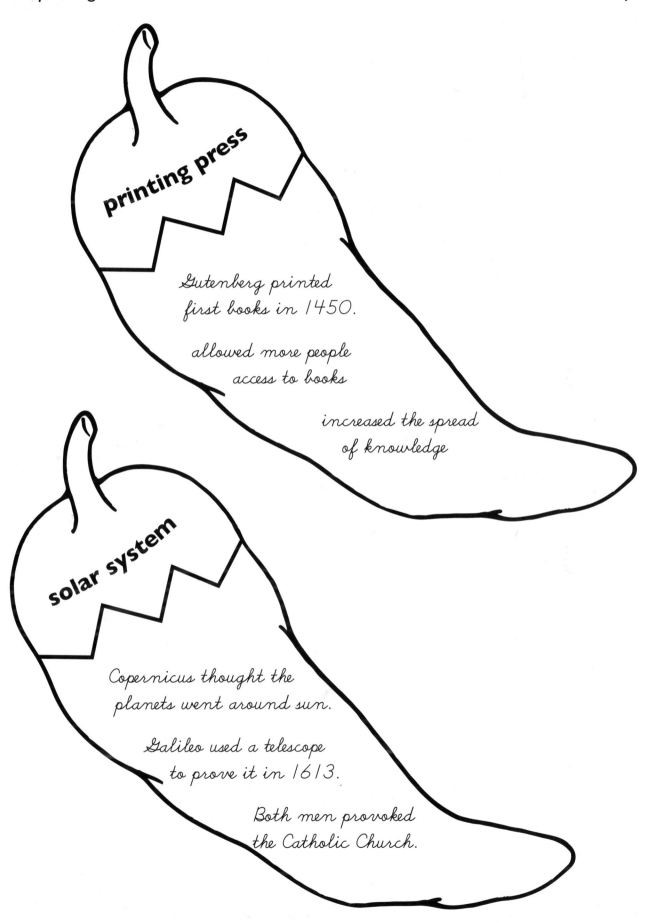

printing press

Gutenberg printed first books in 1450.

allowed more people access to books

increased the spread of knowledge

solar system

Copernicus thought the planets went around sun.

Galileo used a telescope to prove it in 1613.

Both men provoked the Catholic Church.

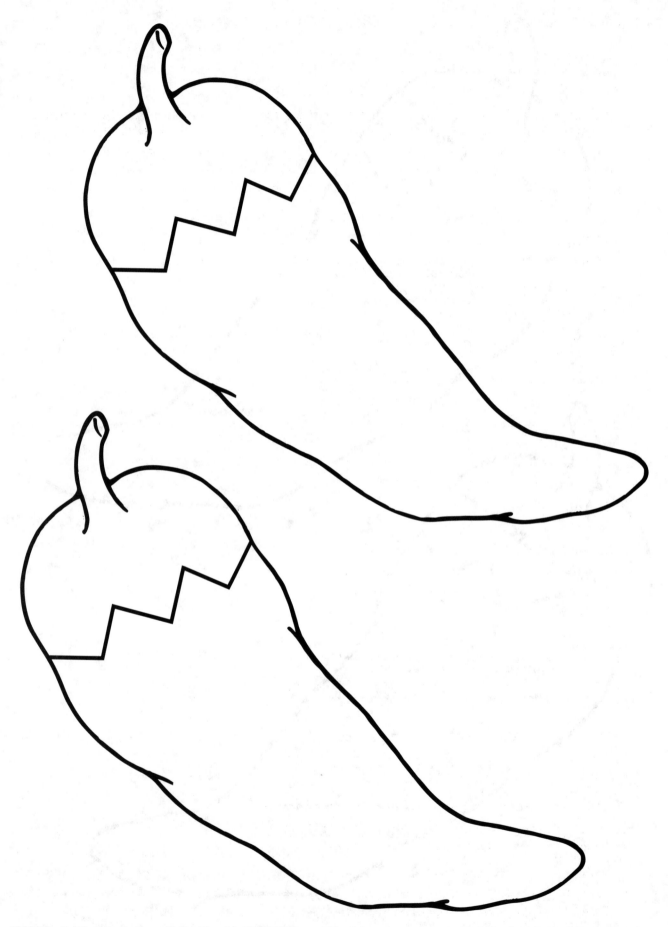

1. Introduce the topic of the American Revolution with the following analogy:

   "Have you ever fought with a friend? Did you hit or shout at your friend? How did your friend react? Did he or she shout at or hit you? Was your fight so bad and did it last so long that you wondered if you would ever be friends again?

   "During the Revolutionary War, the American colonies faced a similar problem. Some colonists wanted to stay British citizens. Others wanted to form a new nation. During the Revolutionary War, the colonists fought against Great Britain. But remember that some of the colonists were on the side of the British. And no one knew if Great Britain and the United States could ever be friends again."

2. Make a T-chart on the board. Here are the questions for the first column:

   - What is a revolution?
   - What kinds of things make people revolt against their leaders?
   - Who usually starts a revolution?
   - What revolutions have you heard of?

3. Discuss the answers with your students, letting them do most of the talking. For example, you want them to define *revolution* in their own words.

4. Introduce unfamiliar vocabulary:
   - **rude**—serviceable but not fancy or decorative
   - **unfurled**—spread open
   - **embattled**—engaged in a violent struggle
   - **conqueror**—winner (of a war, etc.)
   - **seaward**—toward the ocean
   - **votive**—commemorative; in memory of
   - **redeem**—to make up for; make amends for
   - **sires**—fathers
   - **guerilla warfare**—sudden, hit-and-run attacks
   - **tyranny**—cruel, oppressive government rule
   - **tyrant**—cruel leader (of a government, etc.)
   - **ousted**—drove out of a position power

5. Make a transparency and student copies of "Concord Hymn" on page 46.

6. Display the transparency without distributing the student copies. Cover the bottom half of the transparency so that only the poem shows.

7. Read the poem aloud. Next, have students take turns reading the verses. Then, reread the poem chorally as a class.

8. Distribute the student copies and uncover the lower half of the transparency.

9. Have volunteers take turns reading the three paragraphs.

10. Make a transparency and student copies of the "Hierarchy Array" graphic organizer on page 48. Display the transparency and distribute the student copies.

11. Fill in the graphic organizer as a class. Depending on your students' prior knowledge, you may need to provide prompts or just tell the students the additional details about the revolutions shown on the completed graphic organizer on page 47.

Concord Hymn

By the rude bridge that arched the flood,
Their flag to April's breeze unfurled,
Here once the embattled farmers stood,
And fired the shot heard 'round the world.

The foe long since in silence slept;
As does the conqueror silent sleeps;
And Time the ruined bridge has swept
Down the dark stream which seaward creeps.

On this green bank, by this soft steam,
We set today a votive stone;
That memory may their deed redeem,
When, like our sires, our sons are gone.

Spirit, that made those heroes dare
To die, and leave their children free,
Bid Time and Nature gently spare
The Shaft we raise to them and thee.

British soldiers march into Concord.

Ralph Waldo Emerson wrote this poem about the first battle of the American Revolution. It occurred the morning after Paul Revere's famous midnight ride. Seventy farmers took a stand against the redcoats in Lexington, Massachusetts, on April 19, 1775. They lost the battle, and the British marched on to Concord. The men in Concord managed to chase the British soldiers back to Boston through guerilla warfare.

Why was this "the shot heard 'round the world"? At that time most European nations had wealthy royal rulers and a large population of people who could barely survive. France had a long history of conflict with Great Britain, so its king sent troops to help America win its "freedom from tyranny." What King Louis XVI failed to see was that he himself was such a tyrant. When the American colonists beat the best army in the world, the French peasants decided to overthrow their monarch. The French Revolution began in 1789. King Louis, his queen, and many wealthy nobles were beheaded.

The American victory also had an effect on the people of Central and South America. There, Spanish and Portguese rulers had turned the native peoples into slaves. In nation after nation, people thought, "Why should we endure foreign rule? Since the Americans won against the world's strongest military, we will revolt and win our freedom, too." Over time, the oppressed people in these countries fought and successfully ousted their European rulers. By 1830 most of the nations of Central and South America were free.

revolution = a major change in a nation's government or political system

A revolution can overthrow a nation's leaders, form a new kind of government, and/or create a new nation.

American	French	Central and South American

British king levied unfair taxes

ended British authority over colonies

royalty lived in luxury while peasants starved

ended own monarchy; beheaded royal family and nobles

rulers had turned the natives into slaves

ended Spanish and Portuguese control

World History

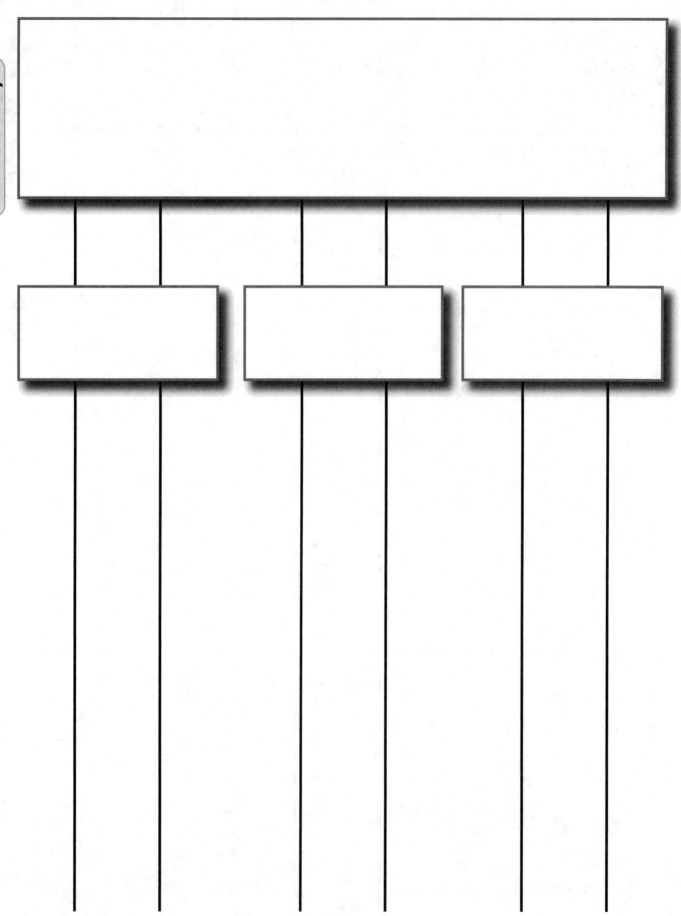

Day 1

1. Have your students point out where Great Britain and Ireland are on a map. Then show them the path of the Gulf Stream ocean current, which has a strong influence on the climate in those nations.

2. Define *famine* (a time of widespread starvation) and ask your students what they know about famines. They may be familiar with recent famines in Africa. See what generalizations you can make about famines. (*They're generally caused by an environmental disaster—such as a drought or a crop failure—or by overpopulation in an area; usually the people affected are too poor to leave. Today there are organizations to help in crisis, such as the Red Cross; such relief organizations are a relatively recent development.*)

3. Introduce unfamiliar vocabulary:

   ✧ **evicted**—legally forced someone to leave his or her residence

   ✧ **tenants**—people who rent land or homes from a landlord

   ✧ **deplorable**—shockingly awful

   ✧ **grueling**—extremely tiring and demanding

   ✧ **exported**—sent to another nation for sale

   ✧ **indifference**—having no interest or sympathy

4. Make student copies of "Potato Crop Failure Leads to Widespread Starvation" on page 54. This passage is written at a 6.7 reading level. Have your students read the article.

5. Make a copy of the blank "Why? Pie" graphic organizer on page 56. Write the three questions shown on the completed graphic organizer on page 55. Then make student copies of the one on which you wrote.

6. Pair the students. Distribute student copies of the "Why? Pie" organizer. Have the partners discuss and answer the questions within the pie pieces. They are to write the answers in their own words and not just copy sentences from the passage.

Day 2

1. Be sure the students have the passage from yesterday.

2. Make and distribute student copies of the blank graphic organizer on page 56.

3. Having students generate their own thought-provoking questions about an article helps them to process the text more deeply. So ask your students to create three new questions that begin with the word *Why* and write them on the graphic organizer. Give students about five minutes to generate these questions.

4. Have students exchange papers and answer each other's questions.

5. Students pass the papers back to their originators. Have the students assess their classmates' responses to their questions.

6. Call on students and have them state one of their questions and the correct answer.

Extension: Be sure to use this graphic organizer with other topics. It is especially good to use as a prelude to writing a research paper, as it prompts students to come up with questions to which they want to find answers in their research.

World History

Potato Crop Failure Leads to Widespread Starvation

Some disasters begin so quietly that at first no one realizes their seriousness. This was true of the Great Irish Famine. A famine is a period of widespread starvation. Between 1845 and 1851, 1.5 million Irish died. It all started with *blight*, a fungus that would kill a healthy potato plant in several days. Then the potatoes could not be eaten. And potatoes were the only food that the poor had.

Ireland is called the Emerald Isle. Although it is as close to the Arctic Circle as Moscow, Russia, its climate is mild due to the Gulf Stream. The Gulf Stream is an ocean current that carries warm water and air from the Caribbean to Ireland. The cool, damp climate is good for growing potatoes, but it is also ideal for blight.

Religion played a part in the tragedy that unfolded. British Protestants owned the land on which Roman Catholic Irish farmers were tenants. They grew wheat and oats in big fields. The money from these crops paid their rent. They also had small plots on which to raise potatoes for themselves. Many other people just worked in the fields. They lived in tiny mud huts and had gardens in which they grew enough potatoes to survive. Unlike grains, potatoes could not be stored for years. Each year's crop fed the people until the next harvest.

Although Ireland was part of the United Kingdom, there had been religious tension between the two islands for centuries. As a result, the British did almost nothing to help the Irish during the famine. Irish farmers and workers had little to eat. Many of the poor sold all that they owned to buy food, and when that ran out, they slowly starved to death. When the Irish couldn't pay their rent, British landlords evicted hundreds of thousands of people from their homes and farms. Eviction was a death sentence that meant slow starvation.

Other crops did well during the blight, but the landlords exported them. The year that the greatest number of people starved was 1847. That same year 4,000 shiploads of food left Ireland for England or Scotland. At last, the British government set up a public-works program. It hired people to build roads and bridges so that they could buy food. Still, most could not earn enough to feed a family, and soup kitchens could not keep up with the demand. Diseases killed the weakened people as well. So many people died so fast that survivors ran out of caskets and stacked corpses like logs in mass graves.

A few landlords paid for ship passage for their tenants to go to North America. Conditions on the ships sailing from Ireland to America were so bad that they were called "coffin ships." The ship owners refused to provide food, saying the passengers had to bring their own. But since they were fleeing a famine, they had nothing to bring. Most people were ill, weak, or starved when they came aboard. Four of every 25 people died during the grueling two-week trip. Their bodies were thrown overboard.

A second famine struck Ireland in 1879. Between starvation and people fleeing, just half of the Irish population was left by 1900.

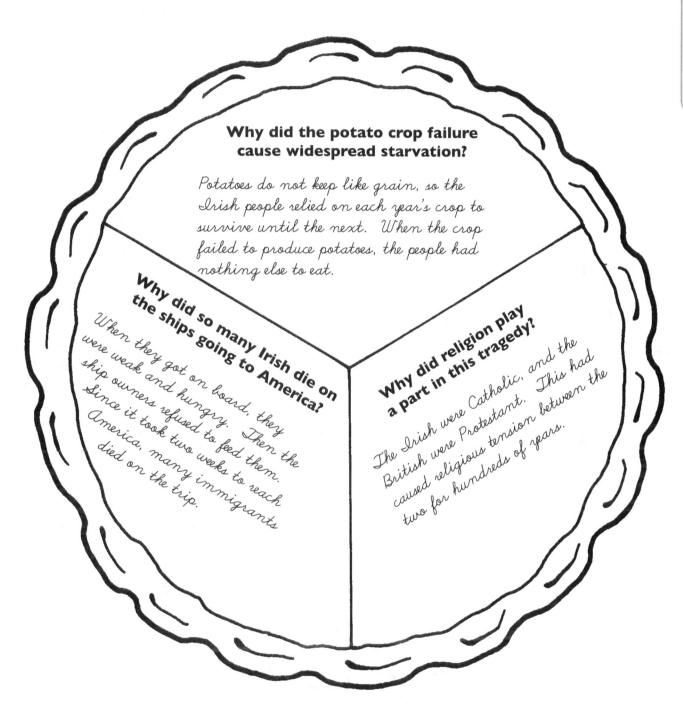

Why did the potato crop failure cause widespread starvation?

Potatoes do not keep like grain, so the Irish people relied on each year's crop to survive until the next. When the crop failed to produce potatoes, the people had nothing else to eat.

Why did so many Irish die on the ships going to America?

When they got on board, they were weak and hungry. Then the ship owners refused to feed them. Since it took two weeks to reach America, many immigrants died on the trip.

Why did religion play a part in this tragedy?

The Irish were Catholic, and the British were Protestant. This had caused religious tension between the two for hundreds of years.

World History

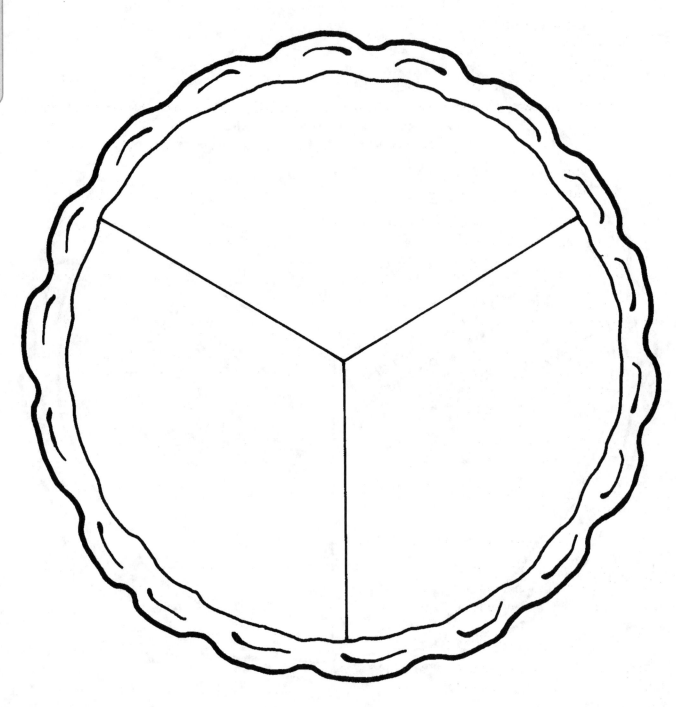

1. Ask students to relate a time when they looked for or followed a shortcut. Why did they want to take a shortcut? How did it turn out? Explain that people have always looked for shortcuts to reduce transportation time. If you have studied the Donner Party, you can remind your students of those ill-fated pioneers that followed a "shortcut" through the Sierra Nevada mountain range.

2. Introduce unfamiliar vocabulary:

   ✧ **rugged terrain**—harsh land that is difficult to cross (because of steep mountains, sharp valleys, swamps, plains)

   ✧ **malaria**—disease caused by a parasite transmitted by mosquitoes that causes a recurring fever and sometimes death

   ✧ **yellow fever**—a virus transmitted by mosquitoes that causes fever, liver damage, and often death

   ✧ **engineer**—a person who designs, builds, and uses structures and/or machines

   ✧ **simultaneously**—at the same time

   ✧ **dredges**—machines that scoop or drag dirt (or objects) from a riverbed or a seabed

3. Make and distribute student copies of "The Panama Canal Changes Transportation" on page 58. It is written at a 6.4 reading level.

4. After reading the article, have your students skim the passage looking for the eight most important facts.

5. Have the students tell you the facts they believe are the most important. Make a list on the board or chart paper.

6. Go through the list with the class. Through the use of questions, help them to narrow down the list to the eight most important facts. Be sure to have students defend their choices. Draw a line through those facts that the class discards.

7. You may need to show students how to combine ideas to come up with the facts shown on the completed graphic organizer on page 59.

8. Make and distribute student copies of the "Steer Me in the Right Direction" graphic organizer on page 60.

9. Have your students copy the most important facts onto the spokes of the wheel.

10. Lead a class discussion based on this question: "Which had a greater impact on the transportation of products, the creation of the Panama Canal or the invention of the airplane?" (Since this is an opinion question, there is no "right" answer.)

11. For homework, have your students write a short (2–3 paragraphs) essay defending their viewpoint.

Extension: You may want to use this graphic organizer several more times with different passages, following the same procedure to help them learn how to distill and combine the most important facts from a long list.

World History

The Panama Canal Changes Transportation

In 1900 a ship traveling from New York to San Francisco covered 15,100 miles. First, it had to go down to the tip of South America. From there, it would sail through the Strait of Magellan or around Cape Horn.

Many sailors hoped that there was another way through the Arctic Ocean. For 400 years, men tried to find a path through the waters of the Arctic Ocean. Some returned frustrated. Others never came back. Roald Amundsen discovered and mapped the Northwest Passage through the Arctic in 1905. However, since ice clogged it for most of the year, it was not a useful route.

The French were the first to try to build a canal to join the seas. They chose the Central American nation of Panama, a narrow country just 40 miles wide. In 1880 the French started to build a canal across it. But their plans failed, and hundreds of men died from malaria and yellow fever. In all, 22,000 men died, many from landslides while digging a pass through the mountains. France gave up.

In 1904 U.S. President Theodore Roosevelt bought the equipment the French had abandoned in Panama. He hired an engineer, General George Goethals, to solve the two major problems that had stopped the French: rugged terrain and disease. Where the land rose, the ships had to rise, and where the land dipped, the ships had to be lowered. So Goethals and his team made three sets of water-filled chambers called locks. These locks raise and lower the water level for the ships. The locks were built in pairs so that ships could move in both directions simultaneously. One ship could be in one lock going east while another ship was in the other lock going west.

At the time the Canal was built, Panama had some of the deadliest diseases on Earth. So Goethals hired a doctor to keep the workers alive. The doctor could not cure malaria, but he did reduce the deaths from yellow fever. Even so, by the end of the project nearly 6,000 men had died.

About 40,000 workers labored for a decade to build the Canal. They used steam shovels and dredges. They cut through thick jungles, steep hills, and swamps to create one of the greatest engineering achievements of all time.

When the Panama Canal opened, it forever changed sea transportation. On August 15, 1914, the first ship, the *Alcon*, sailed from one ocean to the other in just 15 hours. And the trip from New York to San Francisco? The Canal had shortened it by 9,000 miles.

The United States owned the Canal through 1999, and then gave it to Panama. Today, about 14,000 vessels move through the Canal each year carrying 278 million tons of cargo. Panama earns millions of dollars from the tolls it charges ships to use the Canal.

Text on the wheel spokes:

To get from the Atlantic to the Pacific, ships had to sail around the tip of South America.

1880 — French tried to build a canal but failed.

1904 — Americans started to build the Canal.

General Goethals designed a series of locks to raise and lower ships.

He hired a doctor to try to keep workers alive.

1914 — The first ship passed through the Canal.

I chartered the sea trip from New York to San Francisco by 9,000 miles.

The U.S. owned the Canal until 1999.

World History

1. Show your students on a map where Russia, Germany, Hungary, and Austria are located. Be sure to point out Berlin. Explain, "Some of these places were part of the former U.S.S.R. (Union of Soviet Socialist Republics), but most of them were not a part of that huge nation by choice. They were taken over by the Russians following World War II. Hungary was a part of the U.S.S.R. Austria was not. A barbed-wire barricade separated those two nations."

2. Make a copy of the "Active Reading Guide" graphic organizer on page 64. Write the title of the passage ("The Cold War Begins and Ends at the Berlin Wall") on the line at the top. Then make and distribute student copies. This graphic organizer is designed to make your students think about a topic by jotting down a few facts that they "know" about it.

3. Have your students spend about three minutes thinking about what they already know about the Cold War. They may not have very extensive knowledge, and what they do "know" may be incorrect. Have them write what they believe they know in the section provided at the top. Explain that they are to leave the other two sections blank until after they have completed the reading. They are to read the passage, looking to see if their knowledge is correct and what else they can learn about the subject.

4. Introduce unfamiliar vocabulary:

   ✧ **suspicion**—cautious distrust

   ✧ **prosperity**—economic success

   ✧ **liberalization**—the removal or loosening of tight restrictions

5. Make and distribute student copies of "The Cold War Begins and Ends at the Berlin Wall" on page 62. It is written at a 6.7 reading level. Have your students read the article.

6. Discuss the article.

7. Ask your students to complete the graphic organizer based on what they discovered from the reading and subsequent discussion. They must write at least three things under the "New Knowledge" section and another three under the "Surprising Facts" section.

8. Have your students return to the top portion and cross out any "facts" that they discovered were incorrect.

9. Collect the graphic organizers and check for understanding.

Extension: This lesson provided a good introduction to the Cold War. Expand upon it by sharing with your class films, textbook chapters, books, or articles about the Korean War, the Vietnam War, and the Soviet invasion of Afghanistan. All of these "hot" wars occurred during the Cold War. In each case, the Soviet Bloc was trying to enlarge its territory through force. And in each case, the United States and other nations fought back against the Soviets, with soldiers, supplies, and/or military advice.

The Cold War Begins and Ends at the Berlin Wall

World War II ended when the Allied nations won against the Axis nations of Germany, Italy, and Japan. When a war ends, the winners occupy the loser's country in order to establish control. Once things are running smoothly, they leave. The Soviets had fought on the side of the Allies. After the war, the Communist Soviets occupied East Berlin, Germany. Other Allied forces (American, French, and British) occupied other parts of the city.

When the rest of the Allied nations left, the Communists did not. Instead, they renamed the area East Germany. In August 1961 they abruptly cut the phone lines, ended mail service, and shut down the border. No one could go into East Germany, and no one could come out. If a man was on business in West Germany, he could not go back to his family in East Germany. It took some families years to be reunited.

Work began on the Berlin Wall, a 20-foot-high cement wall with barbed wire on top. The Wall had 250 watchtowers and 14,000 soldiers and dogs guarding it. Over the next 20 years, almost 600 East Germans died trying to cross it. The Berlin Wall was a part of the "Iron Curtain." Its purpose was to keep the people under Communist control. It split Europe in two. On the west side was freedom; on the east side was Communism. This marked the beginning of the Cold War, a time of fear and suspicion between the Americans and the Soviets. Each of these world powers felt that the other followed the wrong policy. The United States had capitalism and democracy. The Soviets had Communism and government controls. The Soviets wanted Communism to spread throughout the world. The United States was determined not to let it.

The Cold War was not an open military struggle. But it caused the Korean War, the Vietnam War, and the Soviet invasion of Afghanistan. In each case, the Soviet Bloc tried to enlarge its territory through force. And in each case, the United States and other nations fought back with supplies, military advice, and sometimes even troops.

The Soviet economy struggled under Communism. By the mid 1980s, thousands of Soviet citizens were starving. The Soviet government turned all of its attention to finding a way to feed its people. Then in June 1987 President Ronald Reagan challenged the Soviet leader. He went to a gate in the Berlin Wall and said, "General Secretary Gorbachev, if you seek peace, if you seek prosperity . . . if you seek liberalization, come here to this gate. . . . Mr. Gorbachev, tear down this wall!" The Soviet leader did not act on this suggestion immediately. But when Hungary tore down the barbed-wire barrier separating it from Austria in March 1989, he did nothing. More than 150,000 East Germans left by this route.

Then the Soviet leader announced that he would reopen the border. As of midnight November 9, 1989, East Germans could cross the border for the first time in 28 years. An excited crowd gathered at the Wall. At midnight they smashed it with sledgehammers. The destruction of the Berlin Wall symbolized the end of the Cold War that had lasted for almost 30 years. Today, little remains of the Wall. Germany is reunited, and people move freely throughout the country.

Background Knowledge and Prediction

Before I started reading _The Cold War Begins and Ends at the Berlin Wall_ ,

I knew that . . .

the Cold War took place after World War II and ended with the Vietnam War.

a major battle was fought at a wall in Berlin.

the Cold War was a fight between the two world superpowers of Russia and the United States.

New Knowledge

In the article, I learned that . . .

the Russians built the Berlin Wall to keep people inside Communist-controlled areas from escaping.

the Iron Curtain was a term for the barricades separating the East from the West.

there was a barbed-wire barricade between Austria and Hungary.

the Berlin Wall was built in 1961 and destroyed in 1989; no battles were fought there.

Surprising Facts

I was surprised that . . .

people could not get back to their families if they were on the east side of the Wall in August 1961.

the Wall was so heavily guarded that nearly 600 people died trying to cross it.

the Soviet leader let the Wall be torn down without a fight.

World History

Background Knowledge and Prediction

Before I started reading _____,

I knew that . . .

New Knowledge

In the article, I learned that . . .

Surprising Facts

I was surprised that . . .

Day 1

1. Introduce unfamiliar vocabulary:
   ✧ **destination**—place where someone intends to go or is sent
   ✧ **inhabitants**—all of the people who live in an area
   ✧ **drought**—long period of time without adequate rainfall
   ✧ **descendants**—the blood relatives of a specific ancestor

2. Make a transparency and student copies of "Roanoke Island: Where Did All the People Go?" on page 66.

3. Display the transparency. Cover all but the title. Ask your students what they already know about Roanoke Island.

4. Uncover the first paragraph and ask a volunteer to read it aloud. Have students identify the date in the paragraph and underscore it on the transparency.

5. One at a time, uncover the second through fourth paragraphs, each time having a volunteer read one paragraph aloud. Then, have the students identify the date in the fourth paragraph and underscore it on the transparency.

6. Uncover the fifth and sixth paragraphs, having volunteers read them aloud. Have students identify the dates in the sixth paragraph and underscore them on the transparency.

7. Uncover the last paragraph and ask a volunteer to read it aloud. Have students identify the date in the paragraph and underscore it on the transparency.

8. Discuss the passage. If your students ask you what you think happened to the colonists, do not give an opinion, as this would affect the activity for the next day.

9. Distribute the student copies. Have the students read the passage silently and use highlighters to mark the dates mentioned.

10. Make a transparency and copies of the "Zigzag Time Line" organizer on page 68.

11. Display the transparency and show students how to make the first two entries. (Refer to the completed graphic organizer on page 67.)

12. Distribute the student copies of the graphic organizer and have the students complete it independently. Remind them that the dates are not all given in sequential order in the passage but must be put in sequential order on the graphic organizer. Collect the graphic organizers and check for understanding.

Day 2

1. Write the following list of theories on a blank transparency:
   The Roanoke colonists . . .
   • were shipwrecked on their way back to England.
   • were all killed during a surprise Native-American attack.
   • were almost all killed by a hurricane; a few survivors merged with the Croatoans.
   • merged with the Croatoans because they were starving.
   • split into two groups: one went to Croatoan Island, and the other went to the Chesapeake Bay area. The Croatoans absorbed the first group, and Chief Powhatan killed the second.

2. Display the transparency with the theories. Have students get out their passages from yesterday. Based on its information and their instincts, have them write 1–2 paragraphs stating which theory they believe is correct and why they think so.

3. Collect these papers to see if students gave logical reasons for their theories.

American History

Roanoke Island: Where Did All the People Go?

Did you know that the first English colony in America vanished, and no one knows what happened to it? A group of families went to live on Roanoke Island, which lies off the coast of what is now North Carolina. They arrived in July 1587. John White was their governor. Soon a friendly male Native American named Manteo joined their group.

Not long after the settlers arrived, they found one of their men dead. Fear swept over the colonists. They assumed the Roanoke tribe that lived on the mainland had killed him and attacked their village. Later, they found out that the Roanokes had left, and the people in the village had been a friendly Croatoan tribe gathering the things the others had left behind. Manteo tried to patch up things with the Croatoans, but no one knows if the Native Americans ever truly forgave the settlers.

One month later, White decided to go back for supplies. The settlers promised that if they had to leave the island, they would carve their destination on a tree. If they were in trouble, they would carve a cross above it. When White left for England, he had no idea that he would never see any of them again.

White arrived in England to find war raging between his country and Spain. All ships were needed for battle, so he could not return. For over two years, the Roanoke settlers had no contact with England. At last, White sailed back in 1590. When he arrived, the homes were in ruins. Large trees formed a fence around the village, making what looked like a crude fort. White found a tree with the letters CRO and a fence post had "Croatoan" carved on it. Neither one had a cross. White thought that the settlers had gone to Croatoan Island. He and his crew planned to sail there, but a hurricane blew them so far out to sea that they had to return to England. White never raised the funds needed to return again.

What happened to the Roanoke colony and its 113 inhabitants? Today, scientists know that a bad drought occurred in the area. Crops may have failed due to the dry spell, causing the people to starve. Native Americans may have killed the settlers. Or perhaps they set sail for home and were shipwrecked.

In 1588, the Spanish explorers were in the area, but they saw no white people or dead bodies. In 1607 Pocahontas's father, the powerful Chief Powhatan, told Virginia settlers that he had killed all the people at Roanoke. But in 1709 John Lawson spent time with the Croatoans and noticed that many of natives looked white. Some even had blue eyes, which was unknown among Native Americans. This pointed to the colonists merging with the native tribe.

In the 1800s, the Croatoans changed their tribe name to Lumbee. The Lumbees, the largest Native-American tribe east of the Mississippi River, live in North Carolina. Their oral history states that they are the descendants of the lost colonists and the Croatoans.

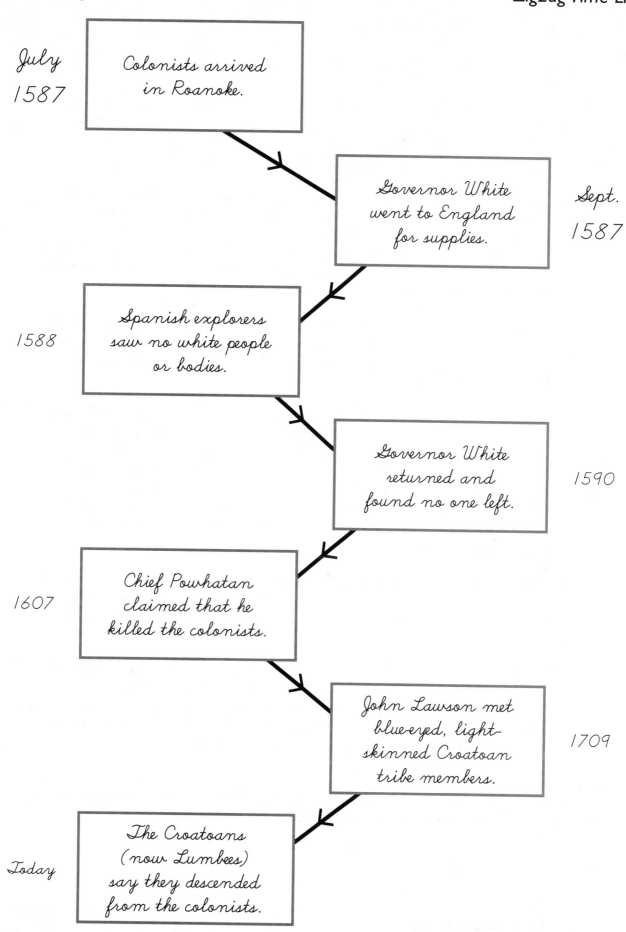

July 1587 — Colonists arrived in Roanoke.

Sept. 1587 — Governor White went to England for supplies.

1588 — Spanish explorers saw no white people or bodies.

1590 — Governor White returned and found no one left.

1607 — Chief Powhatan claimed that he killed the colonists.

1709 — John Lawson met blue-eyed, light-skinned Croatoan tribe members.

Today — The Croatoans (now Lumbees) say they descended from the colonists.

American History

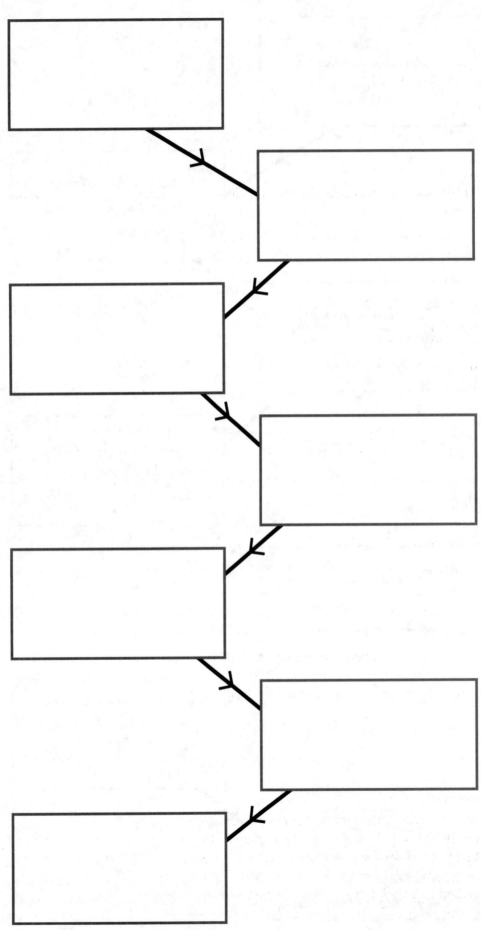

Day 1

1. To pique your students' interest about the passage they will read, write the following names, dates, and terms on the board or chart paper:

September 27, 1777	*6 months*	*Fort Mifflin*
2,000 men	*June 19, 1778*	*Valley Forge, Pennsylvania*
42 days	*General George Washington*	

   Lead a class discussion about how this information will work together in the passage. It's fine if your students make incorrect predictions. The idea is to get them thinking about these ideas and keeping an eye out for these terms as they read. Leave this list up for tomorrow's class.

2. Show your students on a map the locations of Philadelphia, PA; Valley Forge, PA; Fort Mifflin (on Mud Island in the Delaware River); and Monmouth, NJ.

3. Introduce unfamiliar vocabulary:
   - ✧ **pummeled**—repeatedly struck
   - ✧ **ordeal**—a prolonged, difficult experience
   - ✧ **perished**—died
   - ✧ **encampment**—place where a camp is established

4. Make and distribute copies of the article on page 70. It is written at a 6.2 level. Have your students highlight the words you wrote on the board as they encounter them in the article.

5. Read aloud the first paragraph. Stop and ask, "Why did the Continental Congress flee Philadelphia instead of fighting the British?" Give the students time to think and answer.

6. Read the next paragraph and ask, "Why do you think Washington chose to set up camp so close to Philadelphia?"

7. Read the next paragraph and ask, "About how long did the troops at Fort Mifflin anticipate having to hold off the British?"

8. Have the students make two predictions about the remainder of the passage and finish reading it on their own.

9. Make a transparency and two copies for each student of the "Crosshatch" graphic organizer on page 72. Display the transparency and distribute all of the copies.

10. As a class, find the important events in the passage and record them in chronological order. One event affected the next, like threads in a weaving loom. The crosshatching on the graphic organizer represents this. There are 12 total events; so wipe the transparency clean and fill it out twice.

Day 2

1. As a class, review the list of eight terms written on the board. This time they know how the terms go together. Have them work in pairs to write a brief essay using all of the terms. Each term must be underscored in the essay. Here is an example:

   The British took over Philadelphia, Pennsylvania, on September 27, 1777. Fort Mifflin stood between the British supply ships and their troops. The British bombed Fort Mifflin for 42 days and wrecked the fort. But by then the river had frozen, so the British could not advance. So, General George Washington and his troops were safe in Valley Forge, Pennsylvania. Although 2,000 men died in Valley Forge, when the colonial troops emerged after 6 months on June 19, 1778, they were able to immediately defeat the British in a major battle.

American History

American Revolution Heroes:
The Fort Mifflin Troops and the Continental Army

Have you ever heard of Fort Mifflin? Few people have. Yet without it and the men who fought there, there may not have been a United States. The British had built this small, crude fort on Mud Island in the Delaware River. After the Revolutionary War began in April 1775, American patriots took over the fort. When the British marched into the patriots' capital of Philadelphia, Pennsylvania, on September 27, 1777, the Continental Congress fled to New York City.

General George Washington hated leaving Philadelphia in British hands, but he had no choice. The Continental Army was not ready to defeat them. Most of his 12,000 men were untrained in battle. Many had inadequate clothes and guns. Washington needed time to train them. He chose to spend the winter just 20 miles away in Valley Forge, Pennsylvania. His troops started setting up camp there on December 19, 1777.

The British troops in Philadelphia needed supplies. Ships planned to sail up the Delaware River and bring them food, medicine, warm clothing, and ammunition. But Fort Mifflin stood in their way. The brave men inside Fort Mifflin knew that they had to stop the supply ships even though it would probably cost them their lives. In mid-October the British ships opened fire on the little fort. By October 29 the Americans were running low on ammunition. Rainy weather caused flooding, and sewage backed up into the fort. Many men fell ill. But the troops at Fort Mifflin would not give up.

The British knew that after the Delaware River froze, they could not resupply their troops. So, on November 10, three British ships aimed a total of 158 cannons at Fort Mifflin. They pummeled the fort 24 hours a day for 42 days. The men within the fort endured an awful ordeal. They were cold, hungry, sick, and lacked supplies. By Christmas Eve, the fort was ruined. Few of its defenders had survived. Yet their sacrifice changed history. The river had frozen, so the British troops did not get the supplies to attack Valley Forge. Instead, many of the British in Philadelphia moved south.

Meanwhile, Washington had his men cut, haul, and place enough logs to build 2,000 cabins. His officers lived in nearby houses. But this doesn't mean that the owners gladly shared their homes. Many wanted to stay out of the war, and some even sympathized with the British.

That winter cold and hunger took its toll. Sickness was the deadliest enemy. Two-thirds of the 2,000 men who perished in Valley Forge did so from illness. For each man who died in battle, another 10 died from disease. Food was scarce. To add to the Army's problems, area storeowners would rather sell supplies for British money than the near-worthless Continental currency. But the men of the Continental Army rose above these hardships. They drilled and became organized troops. They repaired cannons and learned how to fire them.

The Army marched out of the Valley Forge encampment on June 19, 1778. Nine days later, Washington's troops showed their competence when they beat the British in the Battle of Monmouth in New Jersey.

Crosshatch

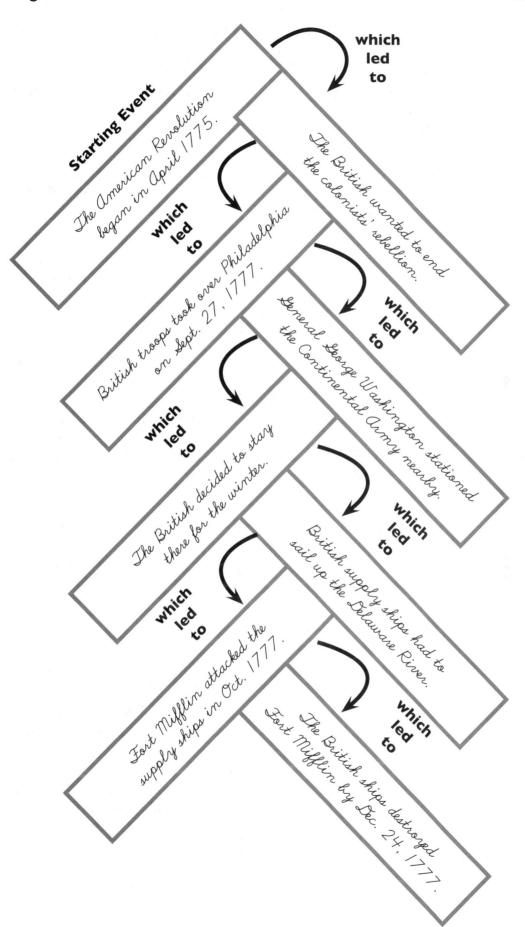

Starting Event
The American Revolution began in April 1775.

which led to

The British wanted to end the colonists' rebellion.

which led to

British troops took over Philadelphia on Sept. 27, 1777.

which led to

General George Washington stationed the Continental Army nearby.

which led to

The British decided to stay there for the winter.

which led to

British supply ships had to sail up the Delaware River.

which led to

Fort Mifflin attacked the supply ships in Oct. 1777.

which led to

The British ships destroyed Fort Mifflin by Dec. 24, 1777.

American History

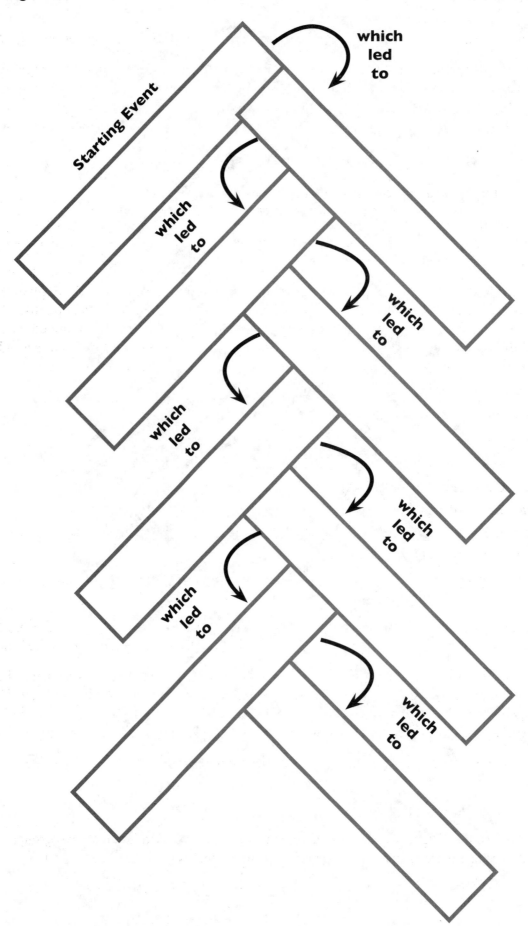

Starting Event

which led to

which led to

which led to

which led to

which led to

which led to

which led to

1. Make a transparency and student copies of "The Right Angle" graphic organizer on page 76.

2. Explain to your students that the way you view a situation often depends upon the angle from which you are looking at it. For example, students and teachers may view tests from different angles. Students may see tests as something challenging, unnecessary, scary, or perhaps exciting; whereas teachers generally see tests as a way to find out how well their students understood the material.

3. Display the transparency. Write *Homework* at the top of the graphic organizer. Write *Students* across the top of the angle and *Teachers* down the side of the angle.

4. As a class, fill in the graphic organizer for how students view homework and how teachers do. Include all viewpoints (e.g., teachers view homework as a way to assess what students understand but may also dread having to grade it). Then wipe the transparency clean.

5. Write the words "Go west, young man" on the board, chart paper, or overhead. Explain that this was advice written by Indiana newspaper journalist John Soule in an article published in 1851. His statement was popularized by Horace Greeley (the publisher who founded the *New York Tribune* newspaper). Greeley published Soule's phrase in the *New York Tribune* as advice to the unemployed men of New York City. It became the mantra for nineteenth-century American migration.

6. Introduce unfamiliar vocabulary:

   ✧ **migration**—movement from one living area to another

   ✧ **enacted**—put into action (e.g., passing a law)

   ✧ **stake a claim**—establish ownership

   ✧ **jeopardy**—danger

   ✧ **enticed**—attracted by offering something desirable

   ✧ **dramatically**—strikingly; impressively

   ✧ **reservation**—a tract of land set apart by the federal government for the use of a Native-American tribe

7. Make and distribute student copies of "'Go West, Young Man' . . . and Everyone Else Will, Too" on page 74. This article is written at a 6.1 reading level. Have your students read the article.

8. Display the transparency and distribute copies of "The Right Angle" graphic organizer. For the title, write *Westward Expansion*. Then write *Settlers* across the top of the angle and *Native Americans* down the side, as shown on the completed organizer on page 75. Students will fill in the organizer based on the angle from which each group viewed westward expansion in the 1800s.

9. Pair the students and have them complete the graphic organizer for both groups (settlers and Native Americans).

10. Reconvene as a class and go over the graphic organizer.

Note: You can use the "Right Angle" graphic organizer for any situation in which two groups may have viewed the same event, situation, or trend in a different manner.

American History

"Go West, Young Man" . . . and Everyone Else Will, Too

Between 1800 and 1880, tens of thousands of people moved west across America. In 1862 the Homestead Act let anyone over 21 stake a free claim for 160 acres. Once a man farmed the land for five years, it was his. Throughout history, land had only belonged to the rich. The idea of free land was amazing. And people heard that there was plenty of rich soil and open land for animals to graze.

To reach the West Coast, people followed trails made by fur trappers or Native Americans. The Oregon Trail was one of the most popular. It went from Missouri to Oregon. It took about five months to travel its 2,000 miles. Some settlers followed the dirt path on horses. Others rode in canvas-covered wagons pulled by mules or oxen. The people packed their belongings in the wagons. They tried not to take anything that wasn't necessary. Still, when an animal died or grew weak, they had to drop things. Over time, tables, china sets, and rocking chairs littered the trail's edges.

Families formed wagon trains of 30 to 70 wagons. The group hired a leader, usually a man who knew the trail well. Even in a big group, the people faced jeopardy. They endured heat, dust storms, and tornadoes. Thieves, wolves, grizzly bears, and Native Americans attacked the pioneers. Illnesses, accidents, and a lack of food took a heavy toll.

The pioneers had to cross the Great Plains and get through the Rocky Mountains before winter, when snow would block the narrow passages. If trapped there, the pioneers could starve or freeze to death. In spite of all of these hardships, thousands of people reached Oregon, where they faced new challenges as they tried to live and work in the wilderness.

Free land wasn't the only thing that enticed people to go west. When a man found gold in California in 1848, it caused the biggest gold rush in U.S. history. People came from around the world. So many people came to California during 1849 that the tiny town of San Francisco turned into a city of 25,000 people.

During the rest of the 1800s, large numbers of people went to other parts of the western United States and Alaska looking for gold. In some places, the mines emptied quickly. Then the people abandoned the towns that had sprung up, leaving them "ghost towns."

Westward migration dramatically changed America. People rapidly made roads, built homes and farms, and created new towns. This caused major conflicts with the Native Americans since it disrupted their way of life. The settlers killed the buffalo on which the tribes relied. They put up fences to keep people off their land. Native Americans did not think that land could be owned.

The Native Americans fought back. But this caused them even bigger problems. The U.S. Army sent troops to kill them. It rounded up the people and forced them to move to reservations—land that the settlers felt was no good for farming. Inch by inch, the Native Americans lost the land that had been theirs for centuries.

Westward Expansion

Settlers

N a t i v e A m e r i c a n s

free land for homes and farms

gold to be found

Native Americans were threats

buffalo competed with cows and sheep for grass

homes, farms, and towns in the middle of their territory

land can't be owned

buffalo killed or grazing patterns disrupted

U.S. Army attacking them and/or putting them on reservations

American History

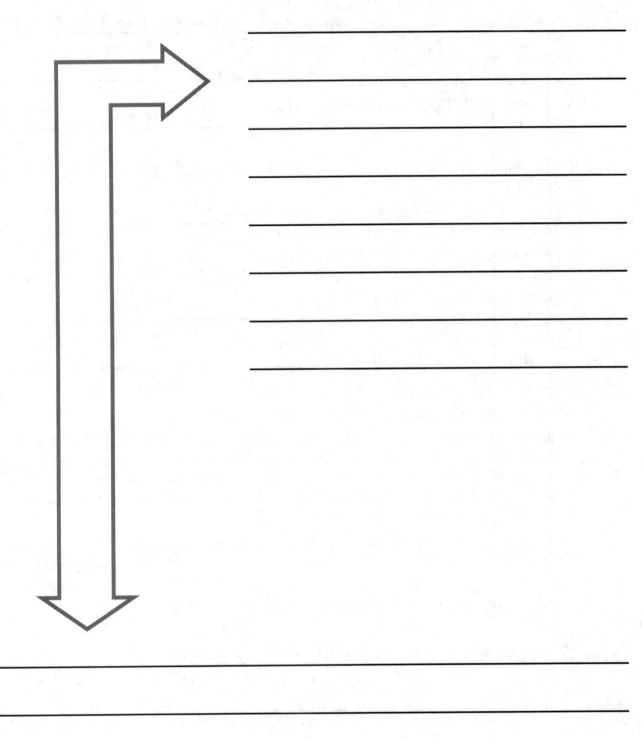

American History

Day 1

1. Make and display a transparency of the "Waterfall" graphic organizer on page 80. Have your students tell you what they know about a waterfall by asking them to:
   - describe a waterfall (*a place where the rocks have worn away so that a shelf has formed in a stream or river*)
   - tell what the water above the falls is like (*rushing, tumbling, roaring*)
   - tell what the water below the falls is like (*calmer, not as turbulent, foamy*)

2. Ask your students to explain how the analogy of a waterfall as a graphic organizer could be used to explain an event. (*Events rush toward a major event (the actual cataract) and then taper off after the climax.*)

3. Introduce unfamiliar vocabulary:
   - **oppressive**—strongly limiting freedom
   - **tactic**—plan or action taken to achieve a specific goal
   - **propaganda**—spreading of information or opinions to help or hurt a cause
   - **persecuting**—treating in a cruel, unfair manner over a long period of time
   - **torpedo**—a long, narrow, self-propelled underwater missile
   - **floating mine**—a type of bomb that is placed in water and explodes on contact
   - **coal bunker**—an area holding a stockpile of coal (which can combust)
   - **furnish**—provide

4. Make and distribute student copies of "Explosion on the *U.S.S. Maine*" on page 78. This passage is written at a 5.9 reading level.

5. Have the students read the article and then discuss it.

6. Make and distribute student copies of the "Waterfall" graphic organizer on page 80. Now that they have read the article, they will more readily understand the analogy it draws. Ask them to identify the waterfall, or climax (the explosion on the *U.S.S. Maine*). The events leading up to the climax are written on the rapids above the falls. The events after the climax are written at the base of the falls. The climax is written on the falls.

7. Pair the students. Above the cataract, they should discuss and list the events that led up to the climax (waterfall). They should discuss and list the events that happened after the climax below the falls.

8. Collect the graphic organizers and check for understanding.

Day 2

1. Have students reread the "Explosion on the *U.S.S. Maine*," focusing on the sixth and seventh paragraphs, which mention the four theories as to what caused the explosion.

2. Ask your students to choose one of the four theories and write a short essay defending why they believe that theory explains what really happened on the *Maine*.

3. If time permits, you can have students do some independent research with encyclopedias, books, other resources, or on the Internet prior to writing this essay. You could also have them write the essay, then do research, then write another essay stating if they still agree with their first choice or if now that they have more facts they believe a different theory and why.

Explosion on the *U.S.S. Maine*

What would you do if you wanted to get rid of your oppressive government? Would you tell lies? Would you try to get another nation to remove your leaders? Would you do whatever necessary to start a war?

In 1868, when the island of Cuba was under Spanish control, the natives rose up against Spain's leadership. In response, the government had many people killed. The freedom fighters continued to rebel without success. Then, in 1895 the Cubans tried a new tactic. They sent propaganda disguised as news to American newspapers. The papers' editors did not check the facts; they just printed the stories. One article stated that the Spaniards had killed one quarter of the Cuban population and then eaten them.

Americans read these stories and grumbled about how U.S. President McKinley wasn't helping the Cubans. So in September of 1897 McKinley told the Spanish government to stop persecuting the Cubans. He also sent the *U.S.S. Maine* to Havana, Cuba. It was the first modern U.S. battleship. Longer than a football field, it had taken nearly nine years to build. The ship arrived on January 25, 1898. Its captain got a note from some Spaniards warning that the *Maine* would sink. He put the ship on alert. Even so, on February 15 at 9:30 p.m., the *Maine* blew up. Since they were in their quarters, the captain and most officers lived. But 262 sailors were not as lucky.

Some people thought that the Spanish had hit the ship with a torpedo or a floating mine. Others said that Cubans did it. They wanted to start a war that they hoped would give them their freedom. Two survivors said that they had heard a cannon blast. Both American and Spanish experts studied the wreck. The Americans said that the ship had touched a mine. The Spanish said that one of the ship's boilers had blown up.

Although the cause was unclear, Americans were angry. On April 25, 1898, the U.S. Congress declared war on Spain. The fighting lasted just 109 days. Spain signed a peace treaty in December giving Cuba its freedom, and America paid Spain $20 million for Guam, Puerto Rico, and the Philippines.

Still, the questions about the *Maine* remain. Did the Spanish cause the explosion to make the Americans leave Cuba? Did Cuban rebels wreck the ship because they felt that the Americans would get rid of the Spanish? Or did the ship's coal bunkers just overheat? Other ships built at that time had that trouble. If a bunker overheated, it could cause an explosion. Yet the Maine had an alarm to let the sailors know if the bunkers' temperature was too warm. It never sounded.

American William Randolph Hearst owned a newspaper. Newspapers sold best during wars. A photographer stated that Hearst sent him to Cuba to cover the war before it began. When the man protested that there was no war, Hearst told him, "You furnish the pictures; I'll furnish the war." Could Hearst have had a bomb planted on the ship? Even today, no one knows for sure.

Events Leading Up

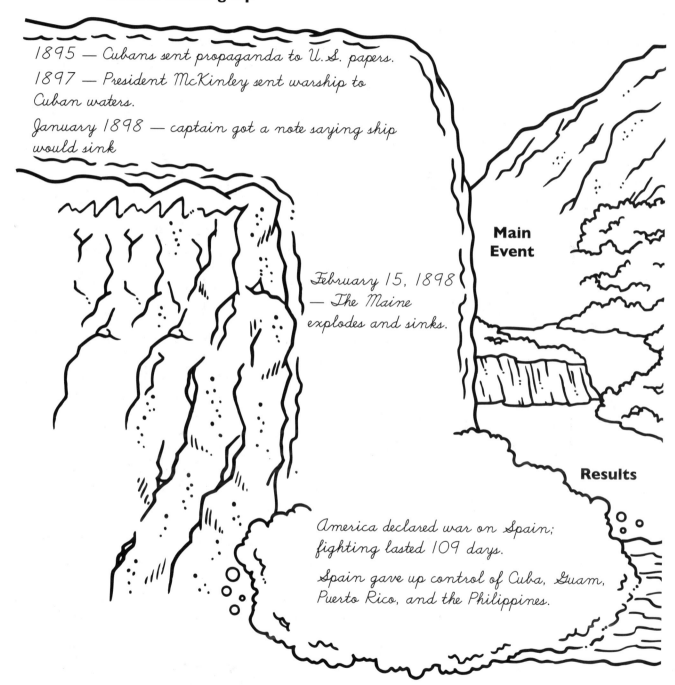

1895 — Cubans sent propaganda to U.S. papers.

1897 — President McKinley sent warship to Cuban waters.

January 1898 — captain got a note saying ship would sink

February 15, 1898 — The Maine explodes and sinks.

Main Event

Results

America declared war on Spain; fighting lasted 109 days.

Spain gave up control of Cuba, Guam, Puerto Rico, and the Philippines.

American History

Events Leading Up

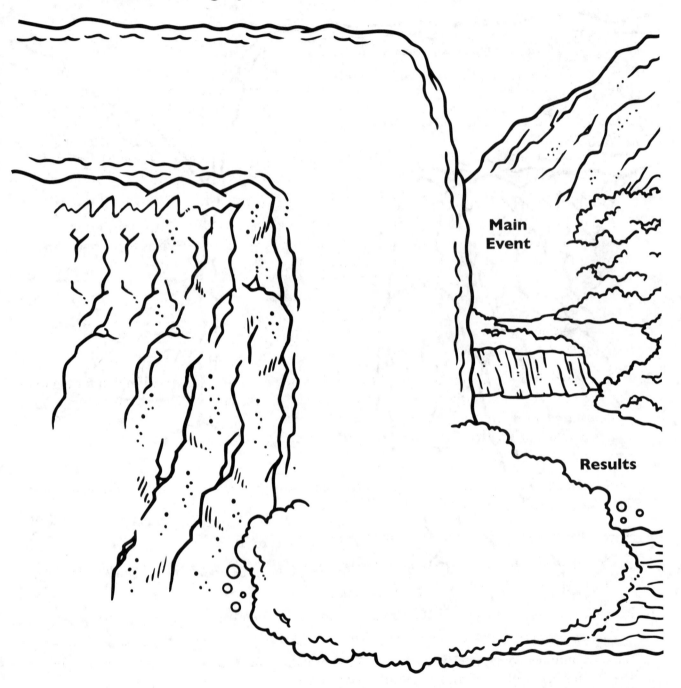

Main Event

Results

Day 1

1. Introduce unfamiliar vocabulary:

   ✧ **entrepreneur**—a person who organizes, operates, and assumes the risk for a business venture

   ✧ **textile mill**—a factory where raw materials such as cotton and wool are made into thread and then woven into bolts of cloth

   ✧ **meat-processing plant**—a place where animals are butchered and prepared for the food market

2. Make and distribute student copies of "Immigrants Fill Sweatshops as Greedy Entrepreneurs Stir the Melting Pot" on page 82. This passage is written at a 5.3 reading level.

3. After students read the passage, discuss it. If possible, have your class read an article written by Nellie Bly regarding her experiences working in a sweatshop. It's entitled "Nellie Bly as a White Slave" and is available at the University of Pennsylvania Libraries website at this address: *http://digital.library.upenn.edu/women/bly/madhouse/madhouse.html#slavc.*

4. You may also want to share with your class portions of Upton Sinclair's *The Jungle*, which describes the deplorable conditions in a meat-packing factory. It's available as a free download from the Project Gutenberg website: *http://www.gutenberg.org/etext/140.*

Day 2

1. Make a transparency and student copies of the "Concept Map" graphic organizer on page 84. Display the transparency and distribute the copies.

2. Write the word *sweatshop* in the center box. Have students come up with a definition for the top box. You can accomplish this by first writing phrases that they suggest. Then, as a group, join the phrases or add adjectives to come up with a final definition (such as the one shown on the completed graphic organizer on page 83). The definition is not cast in stone; use the one your students generate.

3. As a class, discuss examples that can go in the four boxes at the bottom. Then do the same for the "Characteristic" and "Not Characteristic" boxes.

4. Make and distribute a new set of student copies of the graphic organizer.

5. Pair the students and have them work together to complete the "Concept Map" graphic organizer for the phrase *late-19th-century immigrant.*

6. Reconvene as a class to discuss the graphic organizer. Here are some suggested answers:

   Definition: a person who enters a foreign nation to live there permanently

   Some Examples: Mexicans, Chinese, and Europeans coming to U.S.A.; a person fleeing poverty looking for better life; a victim of greedy businessmen

   Characteristics: poor, perhaps penniless; willing to work any job; disliked by American workers; often does not know English

   Not Characteristics: wealthy, picky about employment, treated well by boss and other workers, well educated

American History

Immigrants Fill Sweatshops as Greedy Entrepreneurs Stir the Melting Pot

American factories were growing fast in the late 1800s. But most business owners were greedy men who abused their workers. They set up sweatshops. These places lived up to their names. They were hot, dirty, poorly lit, and often dangerous buildings. Inside them, men, women, and children worked six days a week for 10 to 12 hours without taking a break or using a bathroom. Yet the workers did not quit. Why? There were no welfare programs or charities—and so if they didn't earn money, they'd starve. And there were always many other people eager to take each job.

Where did all these workers come from? They were immigrants. About 27 million of them came to the United States between 1880 and 1930. Most were from Europe. Some came from Mexico and China. Since many of them were fleeing from poverty, they arrived penniless and at the mercy of the heartless sweatshop owners. Some of the worst worker abuses occurred in textile mills, cigar- and box-making factories, sewing factories, and meat-processing plants.

Since immigrants would work in any conditions for 60 to 70 hours a week for low wages, American workers didn't like them. They wanted to form unions so that they could present a united front to the factory owners. Then they would threaten to walk off the job in a strike if conditions didn't improve. But they knew that working conditions and pay would never improve if there were always people willing to endure anything just to have a job.

Then, in February 1910, the workers of 13 sweatshops in New York City did something daring when they walked off their jobs. They went on strike for better conditions. One of the affected firms was the Triangle Shirtwaist Company. But the strike failed, and the strikers were fired. New immigrants were hired to replace them.

Just a little over a year later, on March 25, 1911, the Triangle Shirtwaist Company was the scene of an awful tragedy. It was a payday, and paychecks were being handed out on the 10th floor near quitting time. Most of the workers were Italian and Jewish immigrant teenage girls. As they stood in line to get their checks, a fire broke out and quickly swept through the 10th floor. The one door could not let all the girls pass. The only fire escape fell apart when they stepped on to it. Some waited at the windows for the firemen, but the firemen's ladders did not reach high enough. Water from the hoses could not reach the top floors, either. Rather than burn alive, many girls leaped to their deaths. A total of 146 died. A second exit could have saved many lives, but it had been nailed shut to keep workers from taking spools of thread.

News of the fire brought to light the poor conditions under which the girls had labored. People demanded that the factory's owners stand trial. Eight months after the fire, a jury had to decide if the owners knew that the doors were locked at the time of the fire. When the jurors found them not guilty, people were enraged. Yet some good did come of this disaster: it brought about laws that required safer working conditions.

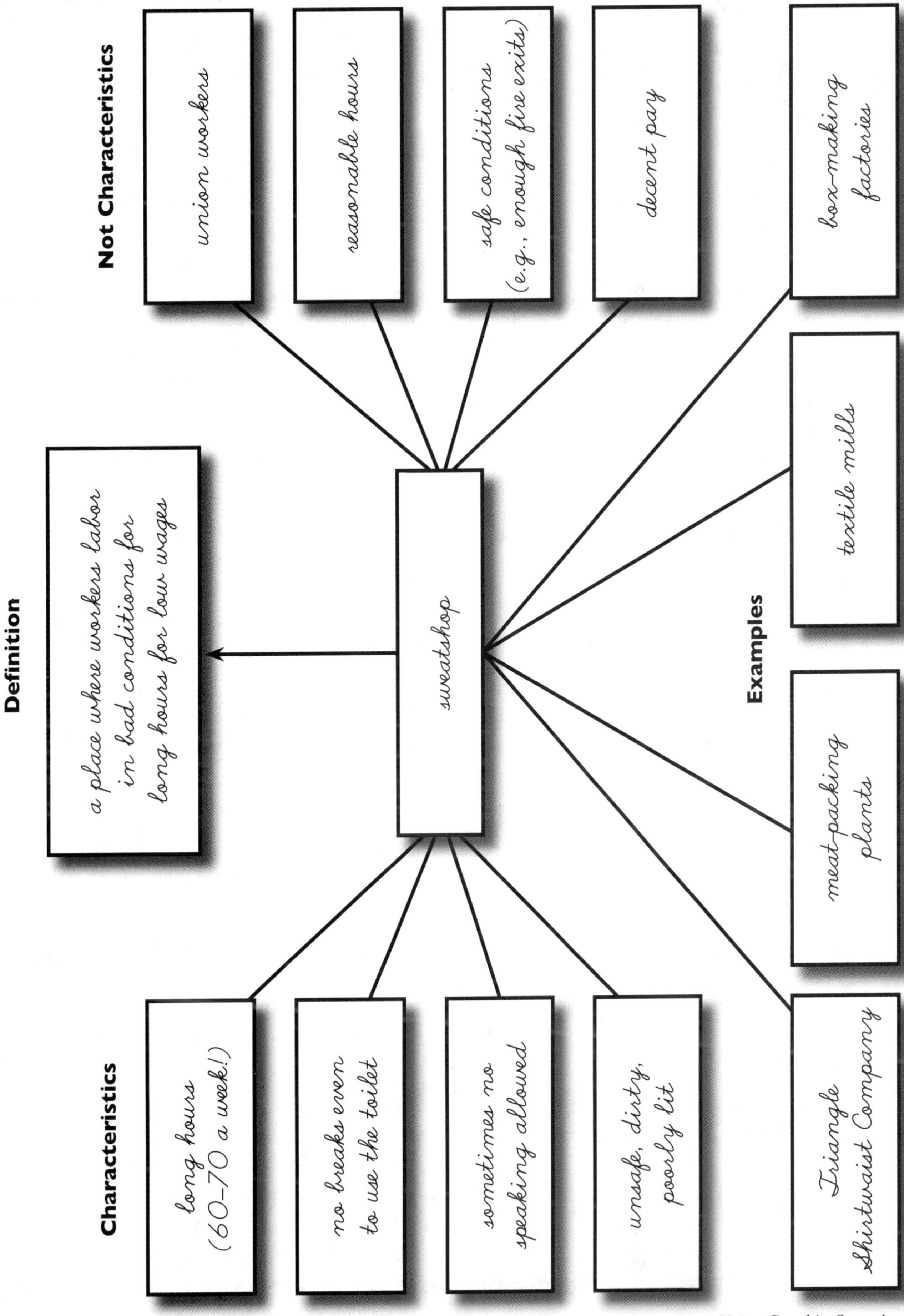

Not Characteristics

union workers

reasonable hours

safe conditions
(e.g., enough fire exits)

decent pay

box-making
factories

Definition

a place where workers labor
in bad conditions for
long hours for low wages

sweatshop

Examples

textile mills

meat-packing
plants

Triangle
Shirtwaist Company

Characteristics

long hours
(60–70 a week!)

no breaks even
to use the toilet

sometimes no
speaking allowed

unsafe, dirty,
poorly lit

Blank Organizer

Concept Map

Not Characteristics

Definition

Examples

Characteristics

1. Introduce unfamiliar vocabulary:

   ✧ **escort**—accompany

   ✧ **U-boat**—original name for a submarine; it's an abbreviation of the German word *Unterseeboot*

   ✧ **torpedo**—to attack with a torpedo (underwater missile)

   ✧ **flotsam**—floating wreckage from a ship

   ✧ **aggression**—hostile behavior

2. Make and distribute copies of "A German U-Boat Sinks the *Lusitania*" on page 86 and the "Life Ring" graphic organizer on page 88. The passage is written at a 6.0 reading level.

3. Make a transparency of the "Life Ring" graphic organizer on page 88.

4. Use collaborative strategic reading, a group activity in which students take on specific roles as they read, discuss, and summarize text. This technique gives the students a sense of control over their own education and works well in classrooms that have students with learning disabilities or English-language learners.

5. Put students into groups of three. Assign each student a role in the group (or, if they are used to this activity, they can select their own roles). The **leader** guides the discussion. The **recorder** jots down any words that stump anyone in the group during the reading. The **summarizer** helps the group to stop after each paragraph and paraphrase it.

6. Have the group members take turns reading the text aloud to each other, stopping to discuss words or concepts that they don't understand.

7. After reading, the groups must restate the main idea for each paragraph in 10 words or less, resulting in a paraphrase for every paragraph in the passage. Have the recorder write these summaries on a sheet of paper.

8. Next, choose to have your students do *one* of these three activities:

   • Tell each group to generate at least four questions and write them on the "Life Ring" graphic organizer. These questions should be higher-level-thinking ones that could be asked on a test and cannot have simple yes/no answers. Have each group decide upon and put a star next to the best question it generated, then pass it to another group to see if they can answer it.

   • Ask each group to generate at least four questions on a piece of scrap paper. Then select four random groups and have them choose their best questions. One group member from each writes the group's question on the "Life Ring" transparency that you have displayed. Everyone in the class copies down these four questions on their own "Life Ring" graphic organizers and answers them as a homework assignment.

   • Have students individually write four questions on the front of the "Life Ring" graphic organizer and their answers on the back. Collect these graphic organizers and use the students' own questions to write a quiz for the next day. This will let the students feel empowered and involved in the evaluation process.

American History

A German U-Boat Sinks the *Lusitania*

On May 1, 1915, the British ship *Lusitania* set sail. It flew the flag of Great Britain as it left New York City heading for England. On board were the captain, 702 crew, and 1,257 passengers. At that time, sailing was the only way to cross the ocean. New York reporters had called this the "Last Voyage of the *Lusitania*." Ten days before, the German Embassy had printed a notice in the U.S. newspapers stating that Germany would sink any enemy ship. World War I had begun nine months before. Great Britain, Germany, and other European nations were fighting. The Germans had U-boats with orders to torpedo any British ship. Germany wanted to stop war supplies from reaching Great Britain. Even a passenger ship might hold food for the troops.

The *Lusitania* was one of the biggest passenger ships in the world. It had the typical cargo carried on an ocean liner. But it also held more than 4,200 cases of ammunition.* The ship's trip across the Atlantic Ocean went well until May 7, when the ship neared the Irish coast. In recent weeks German subs had sunk hundreds of merchant ships in the area. Most people on board didn't know this. They wondered why they could not see any other ships. Irish ships were supposed to escort them. But they never showed up. Instead, a German sub fired a torpedo. It tore a hole in the ship and caused an explosion.

Many died instantly. Others tried to get into lifeboats. But the ship rolled back and forth, and the lifeboats crashed against its sides. Some of them smashed into jagged pieces. Others could not be released. Just 6 of the 48 lifeboats made it into the water. A second blast threw hundreds of people into the sea. The ship sank in just 18 minutes. The captain and other survivors grabbed flotsam. It kept them afloat until help arrived hours later.

About 1,200 people died; 128 of those were Americans. President Woodrow Wilson made a formal protest. The German ruler said that it was an error. After that, Germany did not attack passenger ships near Great Britain for almost two years. But Americans were outraged. The sinking of the *Lusitania* was one of the reasons that the United States joined "the Great War" in April 1917.

American troops probably helped to shorten the "War to End All Wars." Still, World War I took a terrible toll. When it ended in 1918, 8 million had died and 20 million had been wounded. New weapons had resulted in the deadliest war the world had ever seen.

The Treaty of Versailles, signed at the end of the war, was designed to punish Germany for its aggression. Unfortunately, it dealt the German economy such a heavy blow that it could not recover and set in motion the events that led to World War II.

* By international law, its military cargo made the *Lusitania* a valid target. But it was many years after the war had ended before anyone admitted to its cargo.

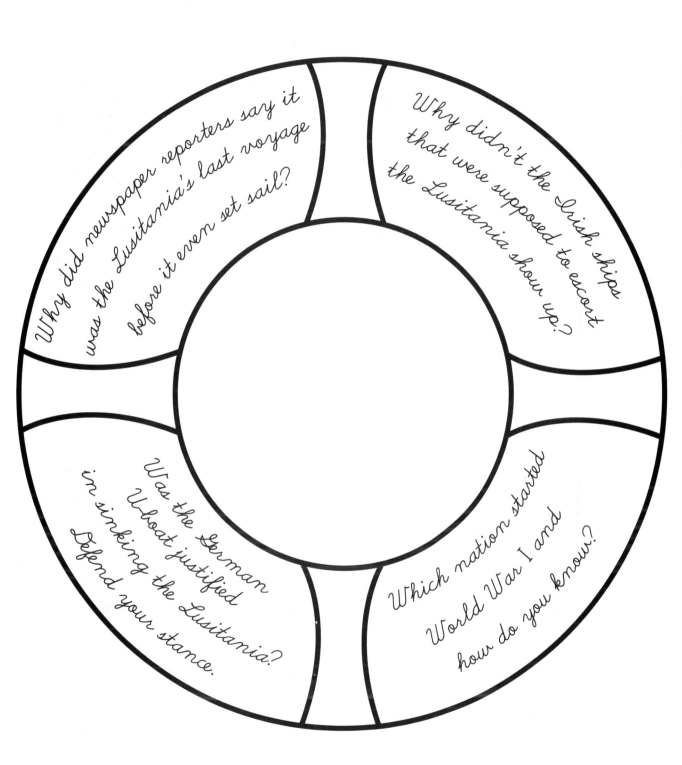

Why did newspaper reporters say it was the Lusitania's last voyage before it even set sail?

Why didn't the Irish ships that were supposed to escort the Lusitania show up?

Was the German U-boat justified in sinking the Lusitania? Defend your stance.

Which nation started World War I and how do you know?

American History

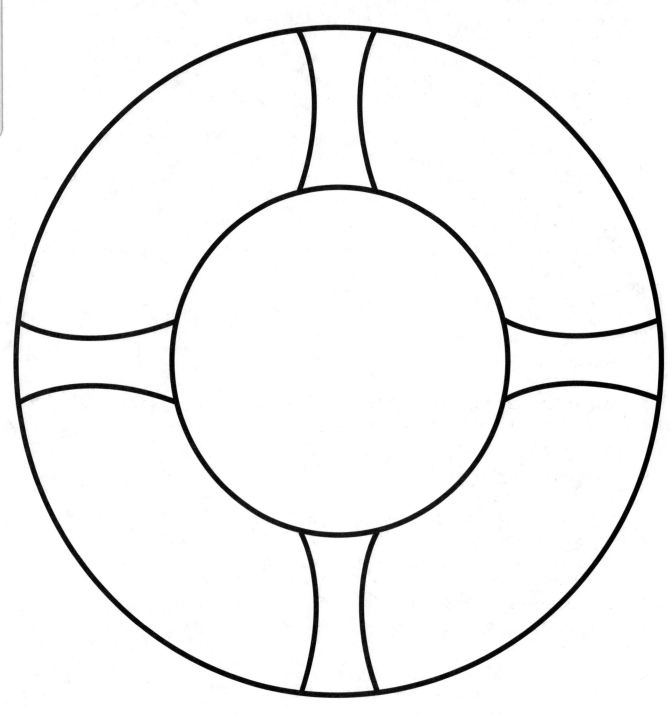

1. Have students close their eyes and envision the scenario you'll paint with these words: "Imagine that America has been attacked by an enemy nation. How would you feel?" Stop and allow some discussion of how students would feel and think if this occurred.

2. Then have them close their eyes again, and continue with, "About 10 weeks after the attack, armed soldiers knock on your door. They tell you and the rest of your family to get your things. You can only take what you can carry. What would you pack? What would you think? Would you ask any questions? What would they be? You are led to a truck. You clutch your backpack as you are crowded into the back of an army truck with many of your neighbors. Everyone looks frightened and confused. No one knows for sure what's going on."

3. Have your students open their eyes. Tell them that this really did happen to American citizens living in the western part of the nation about 65 years ago. They were taken to camps and held there for years until the government released them. They had done nothing wrong, and they were not criminals. They were imprisoned due to their ethnicity.

4. Introduce unfamiliar vocabulary:
   - **internment**—confinement, especially during wartime
   - **suspicious**—distrustful; feeling that a person may be guilty of a crime or threat
   - **patriotic**—devoted to one's own country
   - **descent**—a person's origin
   - **makeshift**—thrown together hastily
   - **barracks**—group of buildings for housing soldiers
   - **real estate**—property held in the form of land or buildings (as opposed to personal property, such as a stamp collection)

5. Make and distribute student copies of "Japanese Americans Confined During World War II" on page 90. The passage is written at a 6.0 reading level.

6. When they've finished reading, raise these questions in a class discussion:
   - Why weren't Americans of German and Italian origin (the other Axis nations) also interned during World War II?
   - What made the Japanese Americans easy targets?
   - Why do you think the Japanese Americans did not fight back?
   - What other famous "human roundup" from American history does the Japanese-American internment remind you of? (*the Cherokee Trail of Tears*)

7. Make a transparency and distribute copies of the "Foot Notes" organizer on page 92.

8. Explain that the feet shown on the graphic organizer are to be filled in with the most important information from the passage. There should be about five facts recorded on each foot.

9. Pair the students. Have them go through the passage, highlighting the 10 most important facts (the ones that matter the most for them to remember). Circulate to be sure they are on the right track and not highlighting too much.

10. Give the pairs time to record their 10 facts on the graphic organizer.

11. Reconvene as a class and display the transparency. Fill it in together. If students offer different facts, ask them to justify why they chose those facts. Gently guide them to differentiate between extraneous details and the essential facts.

American History

Japanese Americans Confined During World War II

When the Japanese bombed Pearl Harbor on December 7, 1941, they wrecked most of the United States' Pacific fleet of ships and planes. U.S. President Franklin D. Roosevelt said it was "a day that will live in infamy" when he declared war on Japan the following day.

People viewed Japanese Americans with suspicion. They thought that they were spies for Japan. This was true even for those who had been born in America and were clearly patriotic. Within a few weeks, many Japanese-American men were rounded up and put in jail. Their families had to give any radios, cameras, binoculars, and guns to the police. Their bank accounts were frozen. This meant that they could not get their own money from the bank. They could only go out in public during daylight, and they could not travel more than 5 miles from home. It is no wonder that those of Chinese origin wore buttons proclaiming, "I'm Chinese!" (China had been attacked by Japan as well, so no one suspected them.)

On February 20, 1942, more than 110,000 people of Japanese descent left their homes. About 70,000 of these people were U.S. citizens. They could bring only what they could carry in their arms and suitcases. They traveled in trucks to trains. The trains carried them to fairgrounds and racetracks enclosed by barbed-wire fences. Armed guards stood watch.

Each family had a small "room," no matter how many members it had. Most of these rooms had been horse stalls. The only furnishings were Army cots. There was no running water or heat. About 300 people shared the toilets and showers. They waited in long lines for meals. The Japanese Americans spent the spring and summer of 1942 in these makeshift quarters. Then they moved to one of 10 camps. These camps were in Idaho, California, Wyoming, Arizona, and Arkansas. They had rows of ugly barracks covered with black tar paper. Each room had a closet, a window, and a light bulb hanging from the ceiling. Rooms were one of three sizes. If you had a big family, you got a larger room.

The people made the best of a bad situation. They planted gardens for food, and students went to schools inside the camps, although they lacked books and paper. Despite their lack of freedom, about 800 young men from the camps volunteered to fight. They served in the U.S. armed forces in Europe.

The Japanese Americans lived in the barracks until the war ended in 1945. At that point, they were set free, but they had to start their lives over. Their businesses, homes, and belongings were not returned to them. Congress passed a law in 1948. It gave $2,500 to individual Japanese Americans. This did not begin to cover their real economic losses, especially of those who lost real estate. Forty years later, surviving Japanese Americans who had lived in the camps got $20,000 each.

- Japanese bombed Pearl Harbor Dec. 7, 1941
- U.S. President Roosevelt declared war next day
- People viewed Japanese Americans with suspicion
  - They lost many rights almost immediately
- February 20, 1942 Japanese Americans left their homes
- taken to fairgrounds and racetracks with barbed wire and armed guards

- eventually sent to one of 10 camps in ID, CA, WY, AZ and AR
- lived in barracks until the war ended in 1945
  - their homes, businesses, and belongings were not returned.
- Congress gave them some money for their losses in 1948 and 1988

American History

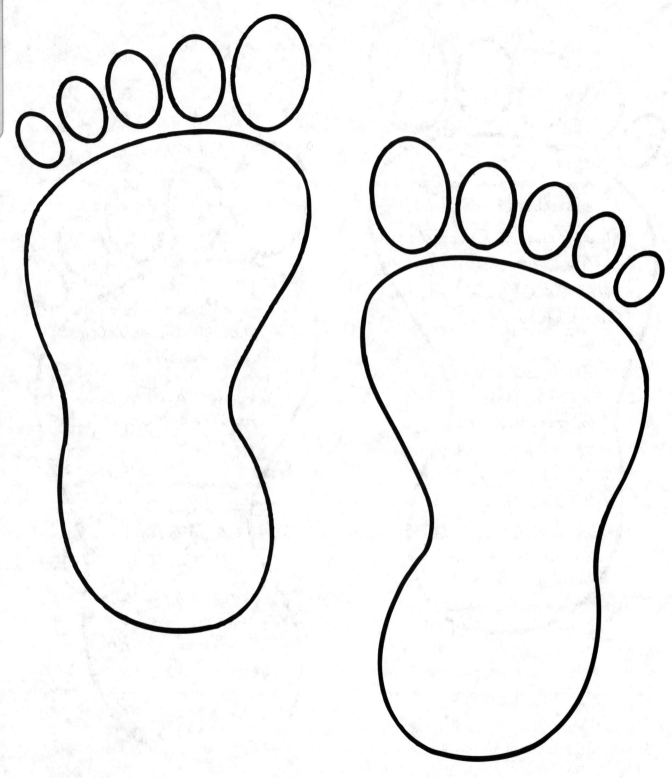

Day 1

1. Show your students where Iran is on a world map.
2. Introduce unfamiliar vocabulary:
   - **Islamic**—relating to the religion of Islam
   - **fundamentalists**—people who strictly follow the main tenets of a religious or philosophical system
   - **Islamic republic**—a theocratic form of government advocated by some Muslim religious leaders in the Middle East and Africa. The penal code (laws) of the state must be compatible with laws of Sharia. In the Islamic Republic of Iran, the Assembly of Experts (who appoints and supervises the Supreme Leader), the president, and members of the parliament are elected by citizens' votes. Only candidates approved by the Guardian Council are allowed to run for election. It's like a republic but heavily based upon religious beliefs.
   - **embassy**—the official offices of an ambassador (a diplomat sent by his or her nation to be a representative of that nation in a foreign land)
   - **captivity**—held against one's will
3. Make and distribute student copies of "American Hostages in Iran" on page 94. This passage is written at a 6.7 reading level.
4. Read and discuss the article with the class.
5. Make a transparency and student copies of the "Sum-It-Up Chart" graphic organizer on page 96. Display the transparency and distribute the student copies.
6. Point out that there are three different "main characters" in this passage. Thus, you will fill out the "Sum-It-Up Chart" graphic organizer three times—once in each column. This will provide a comprehensive overview of the article.
7. Write "Ayatollah Khomeini" in the first column heading. Use the questions that head each row to get your students to tell you the answers needed for the rest of that column. Explain that not every row will have information in every column.
8. Pair the students. Have them write "about 300 university students" at the top of the second column and then work together to fill in the rest of that column.
9. Have students independently fill out the third column for President Jimmy Carter. Remind them that not every row will have information for every column.

Day 2

1. Go over the graphic organizer. Be sure to entertain all of the ideas that the students may have recorded.
2. Discuss how the students can use the information in their organizers to prepare a summary of the information. The information in the first column should be combined to create the beginning of the summary. Write the first part of the summary on your transparency while the students copy it at their seats.
3. Depending on the needs of your class, you can have them work independently or in pairs to take the information from the second column to write the middle of the summary and the information in the third column to create the end. Explain that the final line of the summary, which gives the resolution of the crisis, will come from the passage itself.
4. Collect the graphic organizers and check the students' summaries.

American Hostages in Iran

After World War II ended, the United States supported Iran politically. There were two reasons for this. First, the U.S. economy needed Iran's oil. Second, the U.S. government did not want the Soviets to take over Iran. The Soviets had already invaded Afghanistan, and they made it clear that they wanted to expand further into the Middle East.

By supporting Iran, the United States also backed its Shah. But many Iranians hated him. Some felt that he was cruel and unfair. In January 1979, Islamic fundamentalists overthrew him, and their leader, Ayatollah Khomeini, took power. The Shah left the nation to go on "vacation" but never returned. Khomeini took charge and turned the government into an Islamic republic. This caused economic problems and strained relations between Iran and some other nations.

The Shah fled to Mexico and fell ill. The U.S. government let him into the United States to get treatment at a New York City hospital. A few days later on November 4, 1979, about 300 university students reacted against the United States. They overwhelmed the guards, burst into the U.S. embassy in Teheran, Iran, and seized the staff. They held them hostage. These students lacked money and good weapons. They also acted without any real plan. Yet they made the U.S. government feel helpless.

The students demanded that the Shah return to Iran to stand trial. Only then would they set the hostages free. U.S. President Jimmy Carter refused to deal with the terrorists. So they blindfolded the 52 embassy workers and put them in front of television cameras. Protesters burned the American flag as they shouted, "Death to America! Death to Carter! Death to the Shah!"

Carter tried to get Khomeini to set the hostages free. He had no luck. So he banned imports from Iran. Then he seized $8 billion worth of Iranian funds in U.S. banks. Next, he ordered warships to the waters off Iran. Nothing worked. The American public pressured him to do more. So in April 1980 he ordered a rescue mission. It failed when a plane and a helicopter collided during a sandstorm and killed eight soldiers.

The Shah died in July 1980. Yet the crisis continued. The terrorists wanted to make Carter look weak and ineffective. Only after Ronald Reagan was sworn in as the new U.S. president on January 20, 1981, did they set the hostages free.

The hostages spent 444 days in captivity. Some were treated well, but some were beaten. Others spent long periods of time alone. Most of the captives went on with their lives, but a few never fully recovered from the ordeal.

	First	Second	Third
Who or What?	Ayatollah Khomeini	about 300 university students	U. S. President Jimmy Carter
Did What?	overthrew the Shah and set up an Islamic republic	seized 52 U.S. embassy workers	tried to get Ayatollah Khomeini to release the hostages
When?	January 1979	November 4, 1979	for 444 days
Where?	Iran in the Middle East	U.S. embassy in Tehran, Iran	
Why?	believed the Shah was cruel and unfair	they wanted the U.S. to return the ailing Shah to Iran to stand trial	to free the U.S. citizens
How?		overwhelmed the guards, burst into the embassy, and blindfolded the workers	• banned imports from Iran • seized Iranian funds in U.S. banks • had warships off the coast of Iran • attempted a rescue

Write a paragraph that summarizes the information:

The Ayatollah Khomeini overthrew the Shah of Iran and set up an Islamic Republic in January 1979 because he and his followers believed the Shah was cruel and unjust. Then, on November 4, 1979, about 300 university students overwhelmed the guards, burst into the U.S. embassy in Tehran, and blindfolded 52 workers. They demanded that the U.S. government return the ailing Shah to Iran to stand trial. U.S. President Jimmy Carter refused. For 444 days, he tried different tactics to get the hostages freed. He banned imports from Iran, seized Iranian funds in U.S. banks, and stationed warships off the coast of Iran. President Carter also ordered a rescue that failed. The hostages were finally released when President Ronald Reagan took office.

American History

	First	Second	Third
Who or What?			
Did What?			
When?			
Where?			
Why?			
How?			

Write a paragraph that summarizes the information:

_____

_____

_____

_____

_____

_____

_____

_____

_____